FIX THIS NEXT
for
HEALTHCARE PROVIDERS

fix this next

FOR
HEALTHCARE PROVIDERS

KASEY COMPTON

BEE WELL PUBLISHING

Publisher: Bee Well Publishing
Page Design & Typesetting: Chinook Design, Inc. (chinooktype.com)

ISBN (paperback): 978-1-7362119-0-8
ISBN (ebook): 978-1-7362119-1-5

Disclaimer:
The information contained within this book is for informational purposes. It should not be considered legal or financial advice. You should consult with an attorney or tax professional to determine what may be best for your individual needs.

CONTENTS

Foreword

WOODFORD RESERVE. IT'S THE WORLD'S BEST BOURBON. Hands down. Well, at least that's what I believed. It turns out there are quite a few more bourbons out there. And some are really damn good.

While it is possible that Woodford was once the best according to my palate, admittedly I never tried much else. I subsequently found bourbons that I now prefer. You too may have your old reliable, favorite, whatever it may be. You may even discover that what you loved all along is easily topped by something you never knew existed.

I was on a Zoom call one evening with Kasey Compton, discussing the unique challenges faced by healthcare providers. We talked about the Business Hierarchy of Needs (BHN) that exists within all businesses, and the unique requirements healthcare practices must address.

Traditional business owners need to care for their businesses as they serve their customers. But healthcare providers? You need to care for your business while you *care* for your patients, the major emphasis being on that second "care."

Healthcare is a unique industry in that clients need immediate and undivided attention, which causes the business itself to play second fiddle. The practice can only get proper attention from you when the opportunity presents itself. Which it rarely does. So when it does, what is the most important thing to do?

Kasey had the answer. She quickly scrawled a graphic for me. It was the Healthcare Hierarchy of Needs (HHN). Over time she has enhanced it and it is what you will discover in this book. Kasey has identified the exact things to fix and in the exact order to make your healthcare business flourish. What you are about to read will bring permanent and proper growth to your business.

But first, back to the bourbon.

As Kasey and I discussed the unique needs of healthcare providers, I took a sip of my Woodford Reserve.

"What are you drinking?" she asked.

We were in a professional discussion, and I had unintentionally let my guard down while enjoying my favorite weekend beverage. Embarrassed, I said, "Oops, I'm sorry. I guess I'm starting the weekend a bit early."

"Ha! Don't be sorry. I love bourbon. I just noticed that the color is a bit tawny. I like a darker bourbon with more of a mahogany color. I find the oak notes are best in the darker bourbons," she said. "Are you drinking Woodford?"

"I am. Wow! How did you know?"

"I know my bourbons."

Kasey slid a bottle into the camera frame. It was labeled "Pappy Van Winkle."

"This one is my favorite." She poured some into a rocks glass, neat. The rich, deep copper liquid glowed at the bottom of the tumbler.

"You know, Mike, most healthcare practitioners are doing almost everything right. They serve their clients exceptionally well. They adequately maintain their business for years or decades. They just get stuck. The problem is, they try to fix everything when they simply need to discover and fix that one thing."

She chuckled and added, "It's like you enjoying Woodford. It is great, but when it's all you know, you miss out on the one other thing that will take everything to the next level."

Kasey Compton impresses me in so many ways. She took her own mental health practice from a zero-dollar startup to more than three million dollars in annual revenue in less than three years. Today, she employs over a hundred people and her multi-specialty practice serves nine locations across Kentucky. And she is a healthcare professional herself. These are amazing accomplishments, but not what impress me most about Kasey.

Kasey has helped thousands of healthcare entrepreneurs scale their businesses through her membership community, Mindsight Partners. I have personally met some of the members and I am blown away by the impact Kasey has had on them. And even that isn't what impresses me most.

What impresses me most about Kasey Compton is that she has created the systems and solutions to navigate all the complexity and confusion of running a healthcare practice—*for you*. She could have kept this secret sauce to herself and just kept growing her own practice. But she feels compelled to serve at the greatest level of all: She wants every healthcare provider to be able to grow their business without worry and stress. She is on a mission to give healthcare business owners what they need to feel entrepreneurial confidence. And she wants it to start with you. Right now.

Those systems and solutions? They all start with what you have in your hands. You see, improving your business is not a random rush to "fix everything." Instead, it is the simple process of fixing the right things in the right order.

Kasey enhanced the Fix This Next (FTN) process to work specifically for healthcare entrepreneurs and their needs. Her adaptation of the FTN system translates Maslow's Hierarchy of Needs into the Healthcare Hierarchy of Needs. With this book as your guide, you will learn to serve your business as you would a patient: Identify the root cause, apply the treatment plan, and then elevate to higher-level needs.

Building your healthcare practice is a step-by-step process. You don't need to feel overwhelmed as you attempt to "fix everything"; you simply need to fix the right thing. Kasey will show you how.

The need for your work is greater than ever, and will remain that way for decades to come. Patients need you. The world needs you. To be of the greatest service, your business needs to grow healthily, properly, and permanently. You will make this happen—not by working harder, but by working smarter. *Fix This Next for Healthcare Providers* is your tool for doing exactly that.

So sit back, read this book, and apply the fixes one simple step at a time. Your business is about to be wildly successful because Kasey Compton has already done all the work for you.

Perhaps we should start with a toast? Thank you to Kasey for writing this book. And thank you to *you* for implementing what you learn. Here's to your success. I think some Pappy Van Winkle is in order. Don't you?

Must-Read Introduction

THIS EMAIL ALMOST DIDN'T GET TO ME. I FOUND IT IN MY SPAM folder by accident.

> Dear Kasey,
>
> I hope this email finds you well and doesn't wind up in your spam folder. My name is Anne, and I am sending this out of desperation. I have a practice in Colorado that I have been babying for the last six years. I use the term babying not to be funny, because it's actually quite sad. Every time my baby needs something, I get it. When it cries, I soothe it. When it's hungry, I feed it, and when it needs a diaper change, I do that too.
>
> It throws a lot of tantrums, and in the beginning, I thought it was normal. It actually made me feel good that something needed me. My kids are grown, I am divorced, and this is all I have. My employees complained about not being paid enough and I came to their rescue. Then I questioned all of the reasons I set their salaries the way I did in the first place. A disgruntled client posted a negative review on Google and my heart dropped to the pit of my stomach. I was doing literally everything for my business and it never seemed to be enough. It felt like the more I did, the more it needed.

For the last six years, I have sacrificed my own finances, my energy, time with my family, and now my health for my practice. And I just can't do it anymore. As I type this email, I'm home for the first time in four weeks. I've been in the hospital because I was diagnosed with a rare autoimmune disease and my body started to malfunction. The doctors think the stress of "work" was the catalyst for my disease. I don't know if that's true, but I don't know about anything anymore. I'm emailing with my last ounce of hope. I need help. I need a plan to save my business. I almost said my baby, but I forced myself to stop. I know it's time I treat this thing like a business and not an offspring.

I heard you speak on a podcast about six months before I was hospitalized. I loved your story of how you designed your business and built your team and, most of all, how I could sense that grit in your voice. You didn't have it easy either. I looked you up online, but I promise I'm not a stalker. I saw that you own several businesses but started out as a teacher. I did too. I like your systems approach to running a practice and I'm hoping you may be able to help mine. I need systems now more than ever because I don't have the time I used to. I mean, I do, but at this rate there won't be much left.

Although it may seem like I'm down for the count, I'm not. I still have some fight left in me; I just know there has to be a better way. I'm hoping you know what it is.

Desperate in Denver,

Anne

Wow. Anne's email took my breath away. Anne had listened to my story on a podcast, and I knew that was true because she compared her business to a baby, and I talk about that a lot. I could see a resemblance to my own story in hers, and tidbits of my language in the way she felt. Right away I knew I would help Anne, the same way that I wished I would have let someone help me.

Anne's story came through loud and clear for me because, like so many of us, I sacrificed parts of my life for a business that was supposed to serve me, not the other way around. It broke my heart to read about Anne's illness. I could almost see her working night and day, taking care of her baby.

Maybe you find yourself sneaking in a quick email check… that uncovers a problem… that consumes the rest of your evening. It's possible that you think about how you will attract the highest-quality providers while you're eating your bowl of spaghetti and meatballs with the kids. But we all know it's not supposed to work that way. And even if it feels like it's working right now, it won't for long. It's a trap, and I don't want you or Anne to fall into it.

When I speak at events, I always joke about how healthcare entrepreneurs are content-hoarders. They buy lots of books, immerse themselves in online courses, and troll Facebook groups posting questions, hoping to discover the best of the bestest of everything out there. But they're still stuck, still in that trap. The reason why none of the other gold-nugget solutions work is that they're higher-level. They assume you already have an infrastructure to build upon. They're not the foundational system you need to lay a strong framework. Before all else, you must have a clear, simple, and effective system that tells you where to start.

I used to catch myself behind my desk and realize that I was just working to work. There wasn't anything in particular I was trying to achieve; I wasn't dialed in on creating a system to increase lead generation tenfold, or implementing a plan to increase my margin health by 15%. I was just responding to emails, answering questions that came across my desk, and being present in a business that had lost its way. So many entrepreneurs are caught in exactly the same trap. We're doing just to do, and we don't have a clear picture of where we are trying to go. We don't know what we should be focused on, so we focus on everything.

It wasn't until I nearly hit rock bottom, like Anne, that I realized something life-changing. I didn't need to focus on all the problems. I didn't need to hand over my life so that my business could live. All I needed to do was identify the ONE vital need my business had and focus all my attention on it in order to level up. So that's what I did, and that's what I'll teach you to do as well. Throughout this book, I will teach you how to diagnose your practice and use that diagnosis like a compass. Because then, you'll never feel lost again.

There *is* a better way to run your business. There *is* a way to determine the one thing you should focus your attention on at any given time, based on its level of importance. It's the Fix This Next for Healthcare (FTNH) system, and you will learn to master it. I know you may be thinking, "There's no way. It's never going to help me." But it will. It helped Anne, and so many others I will tell you about. You'll read about how it worked in the stories, the examples, and the anecdotes in this book. In fact, everything I tell you is true. This system works because it's simple and easy to relate to, and it will work especially well for you, healthcare entrepreneur, because you were built for it.

I wholeheartedly believe that your business is just like a patient, and you have to treat it that way. I'm sure there's a troll sitting up on your left shoulder and giving you the side-eye, whispering otherwise, but it's true. Your business *is* just like a patient. It has needs, like a patient; it has one vital need, like a patient; and it can receive interventions, just like a patient. In this book, I will teach you a fail-proof system for diagnosing your practice in order to find that vital need, and I'll also teach you how to create a treatment plan for it.

You will create a plan, just like you do all the time, that includes a diagnosis, baseline, goal, intervention, and plan for progress. Doing this will point all your energy toward making the most impactful change needed in your business. You will see results faster, with minimized wasted effort. This is a tool that you can use for years to come, anytime and every time you need to address a problem.

Even more importantly, I'm here on a mission to help business owners find their entrepreneurial confidence—and it starts with you. You will become empowered as a result of this system, you will become surer of yourself, and you will never let your own business intimidate you.

I want you to feel confident *because* of your background and training, not inferior due to your lack of a business degree. You don't need an MBA to run a successful business, you just need a system that is aligned with your strengths and actually works. Your experience up until this point may have not been ideal, but you can change it. Like Anne, you can make the vital change that levels up your business.

Hey Kasey,

I just wanted to thank you for the FTN course you granted me access to. I'll keep this short because I know you're busy. I can't imagine what it's like writing a book, especially one with Mike Michalowicz.

When I sent the last email, I was at my wits' end. My health was fading, and my hope was too. There was something about the mindset shift that happened when I started thinking about my business like it was a patient. Instantly, I felt a confidence that wasn't there before. I had always thought I was at a disadvantage *because* I was a therapist, but not anymore.

I am working about twenty-five hours a week, and I've learned how to tell my business no. I prioritize tasks based on the Healthcare Hierarchy of Needs, and I never question whether or not I'm doing the right thing. My business still has a long way to go, but at least now I know I'll be around to see it grow. What I'm doing now is manageable, and the stress level that was once through the roof is nonexistent. I love this system and everything it stands for.

Healthy in Denver,

Anne

Words can't describe how this letter made me feel. The validation for the FTNH system, the reassurance that people who use it achieve life-changing impact. That email made everything I've done worth it.

While my goal is always to keep concepts simple so that my readers can process the information and use it quickly, there may be times when it is necessary to slow down, scribble a few notes, or take a moment to mull things over. You may have questions or need clarification and examples. That's why I created a free FTN QuickStart online guide. You can sign up by going to www.kaseycompton.com/ftn. This interactive, insider platform contains an entire mini-course, explainer videos, a comprehensive workbook, and behind-the-scenes exclusives. I know these resources will leave you feeling confident in your ability to treat your business like a patient. I'll see you on the inside.

Chapter One

The Penny, the Pirate, and the Compass

RELUCTANTLY, I OPEN MY EYES AND FUMBLE OUT OF BED SOMEtime in the wee hours of the morning. It seems like all I do is blink and it's time to crawl back in. The days pass by way too fast; morning turns to night, and time practically vanishes before my eyes. Again, again, and again. Sometimes I don't even know how my children got to school or how I remembered to pick them up before five o'clock. More often than not, I don't know what day it is or what time it is. And I'm constantly behind.

Friends, I know you're frustrated with me because I haven't responded to your text messages for the last two days. I get it; I'd be irritated too. People trying to sell me things, there's something you should know. My email is overflowing and I'm behind on everything, so I'm probably not going to call you back about your new life insurance policy. There are only so many hours in the day, and something waits to consume all of them. Time is the thing I can never seem to get enough of.

I'm really sorry, but I don't have time to go to your Mary Kay party because I'm too busy working on my practice's budget for the upcoming year. And there's no time to analyze my operating expenses because I have to sign off on charts, work on payroll, and figure out how we're going to get therapists hired to meet the demand. There's not enough wrinkle cream in the world to fight the battle I'm fighting with my numbers right now.

I don't have time to serve in the parent-teacher organization because I have an employee problem that is consuming my life. I don't have time to return your text about selling IRAs because I'm too busy trying to figure out what it is that even motivates my staff; most of them are barely able to pay for childcare, so long-term retirement plans are not necessarily a priority at this moment. No one is thinking about their future selves right now. We're all just trying to get through each day.

My perspective on busyness and time changed back in the fall of 2017. Thanksgiving was just around the corner. It had always been one of my favorite holidays, but this year was different. This year, I felt as close to giving up on my business as I ever had. My practice was in a bind, a big freaking mess, actually, when I discovered that an employee who had been with me for a little over a year had gone rogue.

I hired her because I realized I couldn't and shouldn't do everything myself anymore. My business was growing, we were about to hit the one-million mark, and it felt like the right time. I told myself that if I could just find someone to submit the claims, pay the bills, and pay the staff, it would solve most of my *busyness* problems. I needed someone who could free me up to be the visionary I had always dreamed of being, someone who could give me the space I needed to be a true entrepreneur.

I was tired. I had spent my first year as an entrepreneur working as if there was no such thing as a clock; I worked for as long as it took, until the job was done. I created manuals, built and maintained the website, and hired all the providers. I was both the visionary and the executor, and I was eager for the day to come when I could get some relief. I couldn't wait for the time when I could actually go on a vacation without being afraid of the place burning down while I was gone. I deserved some help, and my chronic exhaustion was proof of that.

I was told I should work *on* my business and not *in* my business. So I took a leap of faith and hired someone I knew and trusted to captain my ship. I crossed my fingers and wished for luck. This was a big move. I spent the next year training and teaching her everything she needed to know to be effective in the role. Right about the time I thought she was getting the hang of it, she skippered that ship straight toward an iceberg the size of Connecticut—one that would not only change my entrepreneurial path, but cause massive chaos if it were to hit. And boy, did it hit.

On Thanksgiving Day, her position was vacated (putting it nicely), and I was forced to look at the guts of my business, the inner workings, the systems and processes that made it what it was. Up until this point, I had managed to go nearly a year without examining the financial reality of the monster I had created. Talk about vulnerability—this was the epitome. All of my bad decisions, my whoopsies, my three o'clock-in-the-morning ideas were now constant reminders of how I had sacrificed my life for this business. And now, after my Thanksgiving meal, I had to start all over again.

This disaster caused me to question myself as a business owner, my ability to judge a person's character, and even humanity in general. *Is it too much to ask to get a little of my life back? Do I need to go back to thinking busy means better? Does being an entrepreneur mean I have to be a workaholic? Do I have to trade my time for the title?* These were the serious thoughts that kept me up at night. You might wonder how something so simple as hiring a practice manager one year earlier could ruin my holiday and destroy my business; I know I sure did.

I knew what I needed to do, but I didn't have much time. I had to inventory the wreckage, and then I'd figure out how to put it all back together. But first, I had to focus on one thing that scared the shit out of me. Numbers. I had past trauma related to these devilish little digits, and the thought of what I was about to look at caused me to break out in hives. Not the theoretical kind, the actual big, round, bumpy, hurty kind. Accounting software, even something as easy as QuickBooks, was one of the few things other than wolf spiders that gave me the heebie-jeebies. My philosophy was, if I don't have to look at it, I'm not going to. I had someone for that.

Well, I did, but not anymore. The day I sat down in her brown leather captain's chair, at her oversized desk in an empty office, was the first time since my early twenties that I went through the motions of breathing but found that no air came into my lungs. I was immobilized. My heart pounded and I thought I was dying. I was having a panic attack. The room was huge, but it felt so small. All that was left were the nail holes where the pictures that made this look like an office once hung. The room felt sterile and smelled stale. The sun peeked in from the window behind me just enough to show a film of dust covering the bare floor. So many negative thoughts raced inside my head. *Have I been set up? How much did they take? What is missing? Is this all my fault? How could I have been so blind?* And then Vicki appeared in the doorframe with something in her hand.

I looked up from staring into the nothingness; in that moment I knelt on the other side of confidence, begging internally for the strength to keep trying. Vicki witnessed it; she was one of the employees who stayed when the others went with *her* to start *her* business, which was just like mine. She didn't know it, no one did, but I was consumed with fear. As it crept deep into the pit of my stomach, I told myself I couldn't let it beat me. As I sat there with my fingers paralyzed on the keys of my adding machine, miserably confused, she walked toward me with a look on her face I'll never forget.

"I found this on my way into the building this morning," she said as she put a penny, heads up, on top of my adding machine. She let go of it just long enough to tear a piece of tape off the roll to hold it firmly in place. She wanted to make sure it didn't go anywhere.

"You don't need luck," she said in a very soft Vicki whisper, "but I wanted to give this to you anyway." For the first time in a long time, tears welled up in my eyes. They weren't about the penny so much as the fact that someone believed in me—someone with a job to lose, someone who saw the wreckage and knew the battle I was about to face. Someone who believed that I could get us through. And if she believed it, then so could I. In that moment, I started to go from bewildered to bold. She was right: I didn't need luck, but I would take anything I could get.

As she turned and walked out of the room, I realized I was not alone. I looked back at the financial statements sitting in front of me with a newfound confidence. It was like they were glaring at me, daring me to try. But I wouldn't back down. So what if I didn't have a clue what I was doing? So what if I didn't have a team to support me anymore, to help me figure out this big mess? So what if I was basically starting over after two years in business? I sat there, my hand on my forehead, barely holding myself upright, faced with a life-changing decision. I could *give up*, or I could *muster up* the courage to get my shit together.

The problem was, I was *just* a therapist. A therapist who didn't even know her numbers.

Payroll was coming up, my biller was AWOL, and I didn't know the first thing about submitting claims. If they weren't submitted, we couldn't get paid, and if we couldn't get paid, I couldn't pay the staff. Without staff, there would be no business. Even though I knew a solution was possible, it seemed so far out of reach. I had to make the right decision and I had to make it fast. I didn't have time to do everything; I didn't have time for an elaborate, well-thought-out strategy. I had to do what needed to be done to keep the doors open.

Sitting in that captain's chair, I knew I wanted a business that could run without me; I had a life I wanted to live. I wanted a business that was strong enough to withstand all of the challenges we face in this industry. I wanted to feel the confidence that meant I would never be afraid of numbers again. I wanted to prove to myself that it was possible to help people *and* make money, but I didn't have much time. Now, I felt like I had to work even harder—harder than I did during my first year in business. I went right back into busy mode, the way I'd been before I hired the practice manager. I desperately felt the need to repair the damage and regain my pride. That's the thing; when we try to save our businesses, we immediately go into do everything/sacrifice everything mode, and that can be dangerous.

I worked like this for nearly a year after that Thanksgiving. (You'd think I would have learned from my first big business screwup, but I didn't.) I had to reconfigure our Electronic Health Records system and correct all the little errors the practice manager had left for me. I had to find out who was really with me and who wasn't, and get rid of anyone lacking good intentions. And then I had to rebuild the culture of my company and figure out how to put everyone's mind at ease. They didn't want something like this to happen again either.

During that year of rebuilding, I worked from daylight until dawn, until I fell asleep with the computer still on my lap. I told myself that when I got my business back on steady ground, I would slow down. I told my husband that these long hours were necessary, that our livelihood was at stake, and he couldn't really argue with that. He could see the fear on my face, so he wasn't about to tell me to stop. He needed my business to work too.

I made decisions in the moment and hoped they were right, even though there was no rhyme or reason to them. I sought out community because I wanted to know that I was not alone despite the emptiness I felt. I was embarrassed that I had been duped, and blamed myself. I was tired and, to be honest, a little resentful. My trust had been used against me; the person I had once considered a friend had just needed an inside view of how a business like mine worked. After all, that's the easy way to create one for yourself. The countless hours I poured into my business certainly allowed me to earn more money, but it was all at the expense of my family, my marriage, and my health. It started to feel like it might not be worth it. I was in a deep, dark hole and I wasn't sure how I would ever find my way out.

I treated all my priorities as the number one priority, and never left a stone unturned. I thought that spending more time on my business was the way to ensure that nothing like what happened with my former practice manager would ever happen again, so I overcorrected my mistake. I took pride in my perseverance and drive, but what I was really doing was wearing a badge that boldly said "workaholic." When people asked me what I was up to, I felt better when I said, "I am working." I served my business and all its needs until I couldn't any longer, until my body said no more. I started to get run-down. I was tired, I had headaches that never seemed to go away, but I believed my own distortion: *If I don't do everything, I will lose everything.*

Looking back now, I realize that when I thought, *Kasey, if you don't finish this employee contract, your entire business is going to fall apart,* it was just one of the many lies I told myself so I would keep going.

If you don't figure out your financials, you'll have to file bankruptcy, I would say to myself each time I wanted to rest. There were more negative comments, more self-deprecating remarks I'm not proud of. They were lies, and they all came from a place of fear. I was afraid to fail and determined to do everything I could to prevent it from happening.

And I kept telling myself the same lie over and over again: *I am just a therapist. I have to work twice as hard to try and be an entrepreneur. After all, I'm someone who assesses clients, diagnoses their symptoms, and creates treatment plans to help them reach their goals. How will that ever be enough?*

As is true for so many healthcare providers, I found myself burning the candle at both ends. I was so busy before that I had missed the red flags telling me that my practice manager was actually a pirate. Now, when I didn't have the confidence to tackle the most vital need because I didn't know what it was, I found relief in *staying* busy. I still thought that was the answer.

But busy was not better.

My epiphany came when I realized that no matter the multitude of problems I would face as an entrepreneur, in the end, my business was going to be fine. I was going to be fine. There would never be a shortage of needs to address, and there would always be room for improvement. When I realized that I couldn't do everything—and that I shouldn't kill myself trying—I began to give myself a little more grace.

Yes, I was a therapist, but I didn't need to apologize for that. I didn't need to make excuses for my mistakes by saying that my graduate degree didn't prepare me for this life. I was better suited for this entrepreneur thing than I gave myself credit for. I knew my contracts weren't the greatest, but they got the job done. My financials were a hot mess, but nowhere near bad enough to file bankruptcy. I was being so hard on myself, and I didn't deserve it. It was just that I never wanted to be back in that vulnerable position again. I had given my business everything, and it still wasn't enough to prevent something bad from happening. I thought I was protecting it by putting it first, but I realized that what I was really doing was sabotaging my health and sacrificing my life for something that, at this rate, would never return the favor.

This was the first time I saw it for what it really was—a business, and not a part of me. I realized that I needed to let it stand on its own and give it the space to breathe. Even more than that, I needed to breathe too. It wasn't my identity; it wasn't the reason for my existence. It was the thing I created from a passion for helping others and an undeniably strong purpose. It was how I generated income for my family so that we could live life and enjoy all that it has to offer. It existed so that I could give my children experiences I'd never had.

I made a promise to myself that I would never again hand over so much of my time for something that didn't have a pulse. My life's purpose would be for nothing if my business took from me, rather than provided for me.

We often get it backwards. We forget that our business should serve our needs and not the other way around. It needs us to lead it, to direct it, and to be its compass, but not to be its servant. It was important for me to see that my business could be successful. It didn't need a lucky penny—although to this day, the penny Vicki brought me is still taped to my adding machine—it just needed me to show up, be confident, and know it was all going to be okay.

SAVE TIME—GET A COMPASS

I'm sure you feel a lot like I did back then. Tired, frustrated, maybe even a little lost sometimes. You might resort to using your instincts to inform your decisions. You're doing the best you can, but there is no rhyme or reason to what you fix next. You lack the tool that will make things so much easier for you to pick a direction or a starting point. When you can't or won't give your business unlimited hours, just pick up a compass to guide you.

As healthcare providers, we don't use a compass often, if ever. Basically, we are lost and just don't know it. We are trained to assess people and their symptoms in order to create strategies for them to heal and overcome, but we run our businesses using a shoot-from-the-hip methodology, working our asses off and getting nowhere. That's what I was doing when my business got away from me the first time, and again the second time. When I addressed the *most apparent thing* in the moment, what really happened was that I *neglected the most impactful thing* that would move me closer toward my goal because I didn't even know what that was.

I was so focused on the *how* that I hadn't even figured out the *what* and the *why*. I ran my business without a map, without a plan. I had no clear direction of where I was going, but yet I still tried to figure out how I was going to get there. I didn't have a compass to guide me. But you will, and it's called the Healthcare Hierarchy of Needs. I'll tell you about it after a few more words.

Business ownership can be hard, but it's really not that different from treating your patients.

You too might think, *I'm just a therapist.* Like it or not, my friend, you're also an entrepreneur. You may be a healthcare provider, but that's not all you are. You're so much more. You're a helper, a healer, and a problem-solver. You're a lead generator, a cash cow, and an efficiency officer. You're a toilet paper stocker, a parking lot scraper, and an interior designer. You're a job creator, an innovator, and a purpose keeper. You're all these things and more. You take risks and you help people, and you deserve respect for that. You can do this just as well as anyone with an MBA—maybe even better.

YOUR BUSINESS IS LIKE A PATIENT

My Thanksgiving story from 2017 was a pivotal moment in my entrepreneurial career. I realized that I could use my skills as a therapist to treat my business like a patient and make it better. This was no genius strategy, although I wish I could say it was. I had no clue how to put the wreckage of my business back together, so I did the only thing I knew how to do. I did what I had been trained to do for the past ten years. I treated my business like I treated my patients, and it worked.

I created a new diagnostic lens through which to filter all my practice's problems so that I could keep on doing what worked. Just as I did with anyone who came to sit on my therapizing couch, I searched for the core need in all the issues. If I struggled with staff turnover, I didn't just hire more people; I sought out the reason why they left and worked to address that instead. If it became apparent that certain processes took up too much time, I looked for the bottlenecks and congestion points and fixed those. I treated my business as I would treat a patient because that's what I knew. That's what I was good at, *because* I was a therapist.

Just like me, you earned that advanced degree, spent hours upon hours on clinicals, practicums, and internships, and now you're ready. You're confident in your ability to perform clinical work. You know how to assess, diagnose, and treat. You are a healer, a helper, and an advocate for wellness, and now here you are, running a business. You've spent thousands of dollars a year fulfilling your continuing education requirement, hoping to further your knowledge and clinical skills. You are known in your industry for being top-notch. You crave all the tools necessary to meet the needs of your patients. You want to be known as a good doctor, dentist, therapist, chiropractor—whatever your niche, you want to excel.

You may even be the best in the business, and I hope you are. After all, that's something to be proud of, and the world needs more people like you. But if I asked you if you feel as confident running your business as you do treating your patients, could you say yes?

You may never even have imagined that you would own your own healthcare business. Many of us don't start out that way. We don't set out to become business owners and then go to medical school. Typically, it's the other way around: We have dreams of becoming healthcare providers, then we graduate, add those letters behind our names, and start helping people.

At some point in the process, we realize that we want to run a business on our own terms. We have our own valuable ideas, and we want to share those with the world. We want the freedom to fill the void we see in our community, and we have worked places that have inadvertently shown us there is a better way. We buy into the stereotypes of owning a business and believe it's all glitz and glam.

We hang a shingle and then realize it's not as easy as we thought it would be. We are now responsible for ourselves, and maybe even a team that counts on us to pay their bills, keep their lights on, and put gas in their cars. If we fail, they suffer. As former employees, we believe that our former employers took more from us than they should have, when in fact that's not true. You know it now, but you didn't then.

The truth is, as healthcare entrepreneurs, our biggest problem is that we don't know what our biggest problem is. We know we have problems, maybe even lots of them, but we don't know which one we should focus on. This is how I felt on that disastrous Thanksgiving. We know which problem is the loudest, the one causing the most chaos or that "feels" like it's the most important, the one that's like a fire, wreaking havoc on our business. This is the one we listen to.

We rally all the troops and put our best foot forward to shut this bad boy down, but two days in, something new happens. It's urgent too, so what now? We split the troops, delegating half to work on problem number one and the other half to work on problem number two. Then we focus on something entirely different. Now we are addressing three problems, with no idea which one is most important. We're just hoping to calm at least one of them down to the point where it's not consuming the business. This cycle continues for what feels like forever. One thing after another; a new day, a new problem. Before we know it, we roll our eyes and say, "What now?" when an employee comes to us with that look on their face.

Instead of diagnosing our practice and treating it like a patient (because that would be too easy), we treat its symptoms. This would be like someone coming in with an anxiety disorder who reports disrupted sleep patterns, daily panic attacks, and racing thoughts. Would we be effective if we only told them to change their sleeping routines, breathe deeply during panic attacks, and do something different when they experience a racing thought?

No! If we were to do that, we would simply be treating their symptoms rather than the diagnosis itself, and our patient would not get well. We must treat our business like a patient and address the diagnosis head-on.

We must take the "What now?" and turn it into a question we can ask with confidence. We must understand the system for diagnosing our business and addressing its needs so that we don't sacrifice our health or our sanity to keep it alive. We must play to our strengths and use what we know to achieve success.

YOU'RE NOT *JUST* A THERAPIST (OR HEALTHCARE PROVIDER)

A plan is an important part of treating patients, but it's also important for navigating life and business. It provides peace of mind and a certain level of assurance about anything or anyone we come up against, like the pirate. I knew that not everything I tried in order to get my business back on track was going to work, but I also knew I had to try something. My plan didn't have to be a giant one, but a series of small, doable steps that would ultimately move me forward.

I took all the steps I knew to take, read every book I could get my hands on, and tried to absorb as much knowledge as I possibly could; Lord knows, I needed all the help I could get. By 2018, my practice was doing better than it ever had. I worked less, but my business produced more. I had more energy, and my staff was happy. We were helping people, so my purpose was being fulfilled and my heart was smiling. And then I heard about a book coming down the pipeline called *Fix This Next*, by Mike Michalowicz.[1]

I was already a Mike fan and had read all the other books he'd written, including *Profit First* (which changed my life, by the way). *Fix This Next* was

---

[1] Mike Michalowicz, *Fix This Next: Make the Vital Change That Will Level Up Your Business* (New York, NY: Portfolio/Penguin, 2020).

on my radar. I registered for a webinar with Mike in which he spoke of the framework and core message of the book, and opened up the opportunity to become a certified Fix This Next business advisor. I chomped at the bit to read more about how to pinpoint a business's vital need by using a simple tool called the Business Hierarchy of Needs (BHN). What I was doing in my practice worked well, but I wanted to know if there was something more, something that would help me level up. I had a feeling this book might be it.

It was February, and my birthday present to myself was a ticket to a business workshop I'd been dying to attend. I made the quick trip down to Nashville to Donald Miller's StoryBrand Conference. As I sat in the front row, going through my swag bag and chowing down on the bourbon sucker I found at the bottom, I unassumingly scanned the room as I always do. I looked to my left, then to my right, and then I swear on everything, I thought my heart stopped and I was going to die right there in front of all those people. The only thing I know for certain is that my vision went black for a split second. I think my ears started to ring, and if I had been standing, I would have immediately hit the floor. I nearly broke my neck trying to read the nametag on the table to my right. In that moment, I was no longer unassuming. It wasn't a pretty sight. But I was pretty confident: I knew that guy.

Flannel-looking shirt, some facial hair, professional but not overdone—it was Mike freaking Michalowicz, right there in the flesh. He sat two rows behind me and about two rows to my right, just far enough away to make me twist my neck a little too much for comfort.

I tried hard not to fangirl him. I tried really hard. But I can only do so much. I'm not one to make a scene, either, but I decided to stuff my pride into my swag bag, put down my sucker, and get my butt up and introduce myself. Whew! Deep breath. Positive self-talk. By that point I couldn't feel my fingers, but I had regained a slight sensation in my feet, so I carefully walked over. I reminded myself to breathe.

"Hey Mike, I'm Kasey Compton. I met you once before in Chicago last year. We were both speaking at a conference there," I said as I tried to act like this whole conversation was no biggie. He looked up and smiled in typical bro-ish, friendly Mike fashion, but I knew he didn't remember me. I mean, why would he? He's basically a celebrity and I'm a therapist from Somerset, Kentucky.

"I was nine months pregnant at the time, so you probably don't recognize me. I was the one you spilled a cup of water on right before your keynote." He laughed. I still don't think he remembered, so maybe that kind of thing happens to him a lot. Who knows.

I told him I had signed up to become a Fix This Next certified advisor and that the concept of the book had immediately resonated with me. In a very genuine way, he asked me why. I explained that I'm a healthcare provider, and the reference to Maslow's Hierarchy of Needs was a perfect illustration of how a person's needs really are in line with those of a business.

"When I heard about Maslow and your Business Hierarchy of Needs, I knew it was a perfect marriage. I knew that other healthcare professionals would understand this and love the concept," I managed to fumble. The funniest part of this whole conversation was that he listened intently, like it was the coolest thing he had ever heard, and afterwards wanted to record a short video to share with his community. I'm pretty sure I didn't stop smiling or blushing the entire time.

My non-fangirl, play-it-cool attempt: failed.

Although I looked and sounded like a bumbling idiot, I meant what I said. Mike's methodology was spot-on. It was almost like it was destined to become a book for healthcare entrepreneurs, and that I was meant to write it. The BHN was a tool to accomplish what I already knew was important. It was the perfect way to conceptualize something that I had been doing in my practice since Vicki gave me that penny, and it could be perfectly adapted to meet the needs of healthcare providers trying to run a business while having a life. I couldn't get it off my mind, and as I tested my ideas about the possible adaptation of the book for my industry, I found that they worked—and worked extremely well.

It wasn't but one month later that I saw Mike again, up in Jersey, and this time he didn't spill his drink on me. I knew then that the *Fix This Next for Healthcare Providers* derivative was mine to write. And the rest is history.

HOW THE FTN SYSTEM WORKS

A business has internal systems that allow it to function, just like you do. In order to get the most out of it, you must satisfy its basic needs first. There's no way I could expect rock-star qualities from my receptionist if she hadn't eaten for three days, didn't have water, and felt threatened every time the phone rang. We have to shore up our business, create a stable foundation, and build the infrastructure to support the level of pressure that we will soon start to apply with increased sales. The best way to conceptualize this is by taking a look at Maslow's Hierarchy of Needs.

I'm confident that, as healthcare professionals, you will relate to this in a profound way. Just as Maslow's theory says, you must meet base-level needs before you can focus on advanced-level needs such as love, belonging, and self-actualization. Likewise, a business owner must attend to a business's base needs of **SALES**, **PROFIT**, and **ORDER** before they start to focus on something much more advanced, like **IMPACT** or **LEGACY**. This is the foundation from which we function. If you are in the mental health field, you may understand the importance of this model in the way we treat our clients.

Maslow's research is one of the primary reasons that services like targeted case management exist in conjunction with individual therapy all across

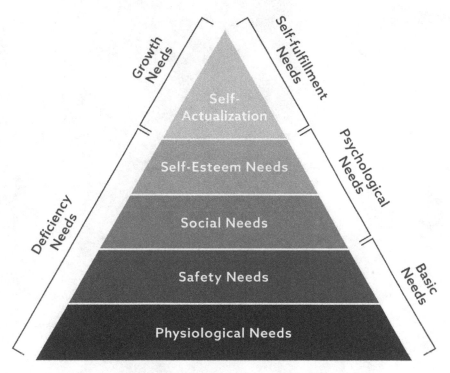

Maslow's Hierarchy of Needs

the United States. It's difficult for clients to achieve a sense of love and be-longing or work toward healthy self-esteem if they are homeless, struggling to find work, or at risk of harm. We must always ensure that their basic needs are met before we can expect them to move toward self-actualization and deeper personal insight.

The same is true for the Healthcare Hierarchy of Needs (HHN) that I developed for this book, a slight adaptation of the Business Hierarchy of Needs (BHN) developed by Mike. You have to strengthen the base levels before you can move up to the higher-level needs. This is not like a ladder you climb, measuring your success based on the height of your rung. It's more like a pyramid. You judge your success by the solidity of your base level. Once **SALES** is solid, you look at **PROFIT**. Once **PROFIT** is shored

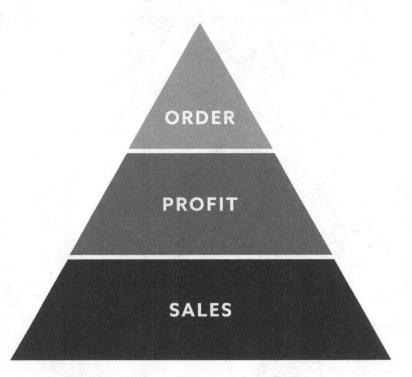

The Healthcare Hierarchy of Needs

up, it's time to focus on **ORDER**. If at any point the sands shift and one level becomes unstable, it's important to go back to that level and make repairs so your pyramid doesn't collapse under its own weight.

The three foundational levels of the Healthcare Hierarchy of Needs are the same as those in the Business Hierarchy of Needs. In this system, though, we're just going to focus on the three where you will spend the majority of your time and discuss the other two, **IMPACT** and **LEGACY**, in the stories you'll read further along.

1. **SALES Level:** This level represents the creation of cash within a business, its primary need. Just as physiological needs come first in Maslow's model, **SALES** must come first within your business.

2. **PROFIT Level:** In this foundational level, the focus is on the creation of stability. Fulfilling needs at this level will ensure that your business does not waver in the face of uncertainty. This also means that in order for your **PROFIT** level to be strong, your **SALES** level must be strong too.

3. **ORDER Level:** In this foundational level, the focus is on the creation of efficiency. Here, your business can begin to scale, and sustain pressure from increased sales as you grow.

Within each of the three foundational levels, there are five Core Needs that must be satisfied before you can focus on the next level. These Core Needs are listed in Chapter Two, and I will get to a much more detailed account of how these relate to your business in Chapters Three through Five. As you begin to assess your practice using the HHN, you will ask yourself the five Core Needs questions for each foundational level. Every no answer to a Core Need question will move you one step closer to getting an accurate diagnosis for your practice and tell you exactly where your focus and attention should lie. **The unmet need on the lowest level of the HHN will be identified as your practice's diagnosis.**

From here on out, the HHN will always be your starting point, your compass, and your tool to assess and diagnose your business. Just to be clear, this tool can be used as often as you wish. In my healthcare practice, we use it at least once a month to ensure that the business is moving in the planned direction.

Once you are confident in your diagnosis, you can also feel confident in your treatment plan and the interventions it includes. You'll be able to concentrate your efforts on the one goal you know will level up your practice. You'll also know that the work you've put in will help build a strong foundation from which to grow.

This sounds familiar because treatment plans are something you use with every patient; after all, they are your jam! When you use the HHN, you will begin to feel an overwhelming sense of confidence about solving the abundance of problems you can never seem to get a handle on. They're like a hundred duck-sized horses running around at your feet. By the time you swat one away, ninety-nine more are coming after you! I don't want that for you. You deserve to feel as confident running your business as you do when you treat your patients.

As we move forward, I want you to remember that sometimes you need to go back to what you know—and you know how to help. You're going to help your business in the same way. You will assess it, diagnose it, and treat it, as you're used to doing as a healthcare provider. It might feel a little strange in the beginning, but before you know it, it will become a normal part of your daily routine.

The point here is this: Your time is valuable, and you already know that. Don't spend it trying to fix all your practice's problems; instead, focus your attention on the one problem whose solution will make the most impact, the unmet need on the lowest foundational level. Use the HHN as a diagnostic tool—as your compass—and apply a treatment plan to make change. When you do, you'll always be pointed toward your true north. Do what you know, pull from your strengths, and find that confidence that already lies within you. You were meant to be an entrepreneur, and you were meant to impact the world. You just need to do it one problem at a time.

BELIEVE IN YOURSELF

As I fervently interviewed healthcare entrepreneurs for this book, I noticed that stories about their battles with time, and trusting their gut rather than relying on proven systems, seemed to sum up the first couple years in their collective journey. Between deciding how to pay staff from a service model and hiring based on the right "feeling," these instincts most often blew up in their faces because there was no system in place to support the resulting decisions. Kayla, of Evolution Wellness in Wilmington, North Carolina, told me that until she started using business logic and making decisions based on numbers, these "feelings" were all she had to go on. (You should know that Kayla is a mental health practitioner, so *the feels* are kind of a big deal.) Once Kayla was able to adopt the FTN for Healthcare Providers system, she relied on numbers and data rather than the gut instinct that had taken her down the wrong path so many times before. As I type these words, Kayla is opening a second location, doubling her staff, and embarking on an entirely new journey whose future consists of systems and confidence.

When you commit to addressing only the vital needs, the diagnoses will change your business. Actually, they will do more than that. They will change your perspective on life. You won't need that lucky penny because you will have a compass, a plan that provides confidence in your ability to be an entrepreneur, not just a therapist and healthcare provider. If you commit right now to taking back your time and treating your practice like a patient, moving your business toward its goal of profitability without ditching your life to do it, I want you to email me.

If you believe that your business is like a patient and you just have to treat it that way, I want to know. If you are ready to say, "Yes, Kasey, I will use the HHN as a diagnostic assessment tool and come up with a treatment plan for my practice," I want to hear about it. Yes, I'm serious, and yes, I mean right now. Pick up your phone—I know it's sitting in your lap—and email me at kasey@kaseycompton.com right now. In the subject line, type "I'll treat my practice like a patient." I want to see your commitment to this process because I am confident that once you finish reading and start implementing, your life is going to change!

THE **HHN** ASSESSMENT

ANSWER EACH QUESTION AS ACCURATELY AS POSSIBLE, USING YOUR PRACTICE'S NUMBERS AND SUPPLEMENTAL DATA

Circle yes or no to indicate your response.

SALES

Lifestyle Congruence

Y   N   Do you know what your billable sessions/services must be in order to support your personal financial comfort level?

Prospect and Provider Attraction

Y   N   Do you attract enough clients to support your level of needed sales for a profitable practice (20% net profit or higher), and do you attract enough providers to support the patient demand?

Client Conversion

Y   N   Do you convert enough of the right clients to support your level of needed billable sessions/services?

Delivering on Commitments

Y   N   Do you fully deliver to your clients by doing what your message promises, following through, and ultimately meeting your clients' health goals?

Collecting on Commitments

Y   N   Do your clients fully deliver on their commitment to you to attend sessions as scheduled, with minimal no-shows and late cancelations? Do they pay promptly for your services?

PROFIT

Debt Eradication

Y N Do you consistently remove debt from your practice rather than accumulate it?

Margin Health

Y N Does each of your offerings have a healthy profit margin, and do you continually seek ways to improve these margins?

Appointment Frequency

Y N Do your clients repeatedly and regularly schedule with you as recommended in their treatment plans?

Profitable Leverage

Y N When debt is used, is it used to generate predictable, increased profitability?

Cash Reserves

Y N Does your practice have enough cash reserves to cover all expenses for three months or longer?

ORDER

Systemization

Y N Do you have an ongoing, working model to reduce bottlenecks, congestion points, and inefficiencies?

Role Alignment

Y N Are people's roles and responsibilities matched with their talents?

Outcome Delegation

Y N Do the people closest to the problem feel empowered to resolve it?

Linchpin Redundancy

Y N Is your practice designed to operate unabated when critical employees are unavailable?

Problem-solving Solutions

Y N Do you and your team have an effective working model for solving problems as they arise?

Chapter Two

Start with the Goal and Finish with Purpose

IN EARLY MARCH OF 2020, I PREPARED MY DOOMSDAY BINDER— the two-inch-thick, three-ring home to the proof of my family's existence. Our birth certificates, Social Security cards, bank account information, and last wishes are all right there between the black laminated cover panels. (I tell my husband it's where he goes *first*, if I die.) Why did I prepare the binder? Because I was about to board a plane for an event and I'm afraid to fly.

Every time I fly, I buy a new book in an effort to distract myself. I'm not often away from the husband and kiddos long enough to actually read, so this was the perfect opportunity to indulge. This time, I chose *The Goal* by Eliyahu Goldratt.[2] Although it isn't as current as other books on my shelf, I had heard good things. It was written in 1984, the year I was born, and is based on Goldratt's "theory of constraints." *The Goal* is big, blue, and full of brilliance. From the very first page, it captivated me. In between moments of catastrophic thinking—*I'm going to die*—I soaked up every word. I made notes in the margins and underlined phrases that struck me.

I never imagined getting so much joy from reading about industrial machines, factories, and metal parts—the three things furthest away from anything and everything I'm confident in. The book has a fabulous introduction, and builds up to its core message in just the right way. In it,

---

[2] Eliyahu M. Goldratt and Jeff Cox, *The Goal: A Process of Ongoing Improvement* (Great Barrington, MA: North River Press, 1984).

Goldratt addresses the effort needed to generate output, how many steps are involved in the process, and how each step is contingent on the one before. Then he poses a question that hit me where it counts: "What is the goal of business?"

I know! I know! I chanted internally because I thought I knew the answer. What's the point of doing all that work? Why do we expend all the energy we have and put ourselves, our families, and our futures at risk? If we commit to producing something of value, then what *is* the goal? Why do we show up to work each day? Why do we skip lunch and come home late for dinner? Why do we miss kindergarten graduations and sacrifice our health to inch our businesses closer to our dreams? *What is the goal of a business, anyway?*

I know the other passengers thought I was crazy as a bedbug, as my granny used to say. I hung from the edge of my seat, clenching that book so tight my knuckles turned white. I talked to it the entire time:

"Yes, this *is* why people are so unproductive!"

"No, employees just don't get it. Where do they think the money comes from, anyway?"

It was as if Goldratt was sitting right beside me, and we were having a conversation about capacity and bottlenecks.

In between my passionate explosions of business jargon, I caught myself shaking my finger at missteps made by the main character. I could already identify with him. I could tell that his decisions were going to land him on a runway that ended in unemployment, divorce, or both. How did he not see it? How could he miss the goal? How did he not see the one thing his business needed in order to remain *in* business?

The goal of a business is profitability. Forever and always.

Goldratt's character couldn't see it for the same reasons you and I sometimes don't see it. He was too close to the situation, too enmeshed in it.

Before he knew it, his role in the company became his identity, and the truer that became, the less insight he had.

The rest of the book built upon this core message and never let up. Learning about input, output, bottlenecks, and capacity was just a bonus for me, because the true takeaway was that I was in business to make a profit first.

I finished up *The Goal* with the validation I so desperately needed to carry on: *The goal of any business is profitability.*

Before I knew it, I was headed back home on that deathtrap otherwise known as an airplane. The bluegrass welcomed me, and I came back to Kentucky with a gift—a newfound sense of confidence and a backpack full of ideas. I couldn't wait to see if my team knew the goal of *my* business. *Of course they do!* I thought.

As each person gathered in our conference room and sat down at the large white table to await the special activity I had planned, I could tell they were both excited and nervous. My heart smiled in anticipation.

Each employee grabbed an envelope with three strips of paper in it numbered one, two, and three. They were instructed to pull out number one, read the question to themselves, and answer it on the same piece of paper.

I kept it simple and asked, "What's the goal of this business?"

After they answered the question, I told them to fold up their strips of paper and place them in the coffee mug going around the table. When the mug came back to me, I eagerly pulled out each strip of paper and read the answers aloud.

One paper read: "The goal of this business is to help people."

The next paper read: "The goal of this business is to be the place where people feel cared for." I knew this was Carol's because of the large, loopy handwriting.

All of the answers were sweet, warm, and kind. But they were all wrong.

My soul was crushed. This was a reflection on my leadership and communication. *You mean they really didn't know?* They all worked each and every day without a common goal. In their minds, as long as people felt cared for, we were in great shape as a company. In my mind, if the business had a healthy profit margin, we were in great shape as a company. Of course, I do want our clients to feel cared for, but I designed the systems to ensure the solidity of that profit margin piece. Profitability had to be the goal, and I needed to communicate that to my team in a way they could understand and would support.

This was one of those rare occurrences where motivational Kasey walks out from behind the desk and stands behind the metaphorical pulpit to give the darnedest, most passionate, most emotional speech she can muster! You see, it's kind of hard for an entrepreneur to tell their employees that this place where they work, well, it's all about the profit. They typically don't respond very well to that. But it was important, and I needed the people who run my business to have a clear vision of its goal. After all, you can't have a practice that *runs* without you if you don't have employees who can *work* without you. And up until that day, they were just working to stay busy, not to reach a goal.

It is my desire for each of my employees to show up to work educated, empowered, and inspired. I wanted them to show up that day—and every day—confident in the knowledge that the goal of Mindsight Behavioral Group is profitability. They needed to know how important their contribution was, and that their actions would certainly move the team one step closer toward the goal or one step further from the goal. I needed them to make the right step.

Up until then, everything was reactionary. If the company had a goal, and each position had a goal that supported the overarching one, how would that change things? How would it change the employees' daily routine? Would it increase their sense of urgency? Would it help the business become profitable faster? The answers here are yes, yes, and yes! Not only did I have to pinpoint my business's diagnosis, I needed to teach my team to do so as well. When you have a group of people all doing their part to ensure the business's goal is met, you are able to show up each day with a greater sense of purpose.

From my chief operating officer-in-training to my front desk receptionist, when my practice staff understood the difference between our goal and our purpose, their focus shifted. They became more intentional and deliberate in their actions. They understood that caring for people *and* making money *was* possible. And, even more importantly, they understood that that's the way it was supposed to be. They stopped doing things that weren't moving the business forward. They reevaluated tasks on their to-do lists and removed those that were unnecessary. When you and your team are able to lock onto this concept, you will see significant improvement in both focus and productivity.

As I prepared for bed that evening, the day replayed in my head (as it often does). I went back through the speech I used to ignite my team and reflected on a few key words that I couldn't get out of my mind. Purpose, passion, and pursuit were just a handful that resonated with me.

My employees choose to work for me—not because they can't find a job somewhere else, but because they care about people and are passionate about fulfilling the business's purpose and committed to embracing its goal. We are all in pursuit of our own purpose; it just so happens that we need profitability to take us there.

EMBRACE YOUR INNER DIAGNOSTICIAN

House was a hit television show on Fox for eight seasons. Its main character, Dr. Gregory House, is an abrasive, unconventional, and callous physician who leads a team of diagnosticians at the fictional Princeton-Plainsboro

Teaching Hospital in New Jersey. Despite his lack of bedside manner, nearly every patient wants to see him. Even if they don't, they need to. Their lives are on the line and they are desperate for help.

Patients live for years slapped with wrong diagnosis after wrong diagnosis, receiving wrong treatment after wrong treatment, and subjecting their bodies to completely unnecessary procedures. As a result, many are left with complicated and convoluted medical histories. Their cases are nearly impossible to sort out, and there is only one doctor who could solve these mysteries: Dr. Gregory House.

Dr. House exists on the brink of termination. His egocentric attitude and unconventional diagnostic techniques precede him. Dr. House has a skill that no one else does: he has the ability to look at complex medical scenarios, the ones no other physicians have been able to treat, and give them a name. He is able to diagnose what no one else can. He sees connections between people and their symptoms in their stories and is able to use process of elimination to apply a differential diagnosis to practically every scenario. Shift after shift, he saves lives, and this earns him the respect of his colleagues. He can diagnose any disease or disorder because he is able to focus on the important symptoms relative to the problem and temporarily push the others out of the way.

Many would call Dr. House a narcissist; be that as it may, he operates with both a goal and a purpose. His life's purpose is to learn, and to continue his quest to solve medical puzzles. In order to learn, he has to understand complex diagnoses and subsequently cure patients, which is the goal. For every patient who lives as a result of his diagnosis, he meets his goal and moves one step further toward satisfying his purpose. Because he has such a strong desire for professional satisfaction and vindication, he is able to go after his goal with great focus and persistence, fervently searching for solutions to some of the most terrifying disease states.

In order to be profitable in business, we must be effective in our craft, just like House. We must cultivate the ability to help people because we can *and* because we care. And because profitability is the goal, we must use these talents and skills to generate the sales that ultimately provide the opportunity for profit.

It doesn't matter if you are Dr. Gregory House, Dr. Smith, or anyone else. You must work toward a clear goal in order to fulfill the purpose that lies within your heart.

THE DIAGNOSTIC ASSESSMENT

As I write this book, we are in the middle of a global pandemic. I have oscillated between anxiety and exhaustion throughout this national crisis, experiencing more uncertainty about safety and security than normal. I was actually boarding a flight when COVID-19 first became the media's top story. Flying *into* Newark International Airport was like any other travel experience, but by the time I boarded a flight back to Kentucky, we might as well have been on the brink of an apocalypse.

People were uncomfortable, agitated, and scared. A chill lingered in the air as I made my way through the terminals to Gate 27C, careful not to miss my flight as I had so many times before in other airports. Only two days had gone by since I left Kentucky, and now it was like I was in a different world. For the first time ever, I felt truly scared about my family's well-being. What would I do to provide for them if worse came to worst? Pretty soon, nothing seemed to matter except for my children's safety and their ability to eat and be well. This was the first time I had ever experienced a true connection with Maslow's Hierarchy of Needs, and I was identifying with its lowest foundational level for sure.

My gut said, "Be ready for anything." Perhaps it was paranoia, or maybe not. Was I being overdramatic? I hoped so. I felt a genuine sense of fear; I felt unsafe. At that point, nothing else mattered. If Maslow's fifth level of

Self-Actualization was a light at the end of the tunnel, I was nowhere close. My physiological being was in jeopardy, so self-actualization wasn't even on the horizon. Has there ever been a time in your life when you were only able to think about your physical safety and well-being, and nothing else? What did that feel like for you? Maslow's Hierarchy of Needs made sense in the 1940s when he created it, and it still applies today.

As a reminder, the Healthcare Hierarchy of Needs (HHN) is similar in concept to Maslow's. The primary difference is in its three foundational levels. In the HHN, you will find **SALES**, **PROFIT**, and **ORDER**. These levels replace Maslow's and give you the framework to diagnose your business. When you know their order from bottom to top, you can determine a fail-proof starting point because your business's diagnosis will always be the *lowest unmet need* on the *lowest foundational level*. An accurate diagnosis is always the first step; therefore, it is critical. You will not achieve maximum profitability without it.

The first step in the Fix This Next for Healthcare (FTNH) system is the diagnostic assessment, the HHN. You can't treat what you can't name, which is why this is step number one. The HHN uses the framework of the three levels to help you visualize and understand levels of priority as you begin working on your business. You will always start with the lowest unmet need on the lowest foundational level. In order to make the best use of this framework, it's important to understand these key points.

1. There are three foundational levels of the HHN: **SALES**, **PROFIT**, and **ORDER**.
2. Within each of the three foundational levels, you will find five Core Needs.
3. The unmet Core Need on the lowest level will become your diagnosis.

We take a much deeper dive into these concepts in the FTN QuickStart. If you haven't requested access online,[3] now's a great time to do so.

Introduction to SALES

SALES is the foundational level of the HHN. For healthcare entrepreneurs, **SALES** equate to the number of clients, incoming leads and inquiries, billable sessions, and services. It doesn't matter who you are or how many letters you have behind your name—if you don't have sales, your practice cannot sustain itself. This is why it is the foundational level.

Here are the five Core Needs and corresponding questions for the **SALES** level:

1. **Lifestyle Congruence:** Do you know what your practice's sales (billable sessions and services) must be in order to support your personal financial comfort level?
2. **Prospect and Provider Attraction:** Do you attract enough clients to support your level of needed sales for a profitable practice (20% net or higher), and do you attract enough providers to support the sales demand?
3. **Client Conversion:** Do you convert enough of the right clients to support your level of needed sales?
4. **Delivering on Commitments:** Do you fully deliver on your commitments to your clients?
5. **Collecting on Commitments:** Do your clients fully deliver on their commitments to you?

---

[3] https://www.kaseycompton.com/ftn

Introduction to PROFIT

PROFIT is the second level of the HHN, and it's where we start to focus on the creation of stability. It doesn't matter how much you have in sales—without profit, it's all for nothing. When all five Core Needs in the **PROFIT** level are satisfied, it means you have minimized your risk of financial implosion and are ready to reassess and possibly move up to the next level.

Here are the five Core Needs and corresponding questions for the **PROFIT** level:

1. **Debt Eradication:** Do you consistently remove debt rather than accumulate it?
2. **Margin Health:** Does each of your offerings have a healthy profit margin, and do you continually seek ways to improve these margins?
3. **Appointment Frequency:** Do your clients repeatedly and regularly schedule with you as recommended in their treatment plans?
4. **Profitable Leverage:** When debt is used, is it used to generate predictable, increased profitability?
5. **Cash Reserves:** Does your practice have enough cash reserves to cover all expenses for three months or longer?

Introduction to ORDER

At this level, the focus is on the creation of efficiency, and the needs are related to ensuring that your business can run without you. When you create **ORDER**, you will find a confidence within that you may never have known before. You will find peace and freedom. As an entrepreneur, you deserve this. Heck, that's why most of us decided to endure the hell we pay as business owners! The freedom to write our own rules calls to the heartstrings of a true entrepreneur.

Here are the five Core Needs and corresponding questions for the **ORDER** level:

1. **Systemization:** Do you have an ongoing, working model to reduce bottlenecks, congestion points, and inefficiencies?
2. **Role Alignment:** Are people's roles and responsibilities matched with their talents?
3. **Outcome Delegation:** Do the people closest to the problem feel empowered to resolve it?
4. **Linchpin Redundancy:** Is your practice designed to operate unabated when critical employees are unavailable?
5. **Problem-solving Solutions:** Do you and your team have an effective working model for solving problems as they arise?

Before we go any further, it's important to understand that the HHN assessment is a tool to help you determine what to fix next and does not represent the state of a business's growth. For example, you don't necessarily start at **SALES**, move your way up to **PROFIT**, and graduate to **ORDER**. The HHN is designed to be the tool that helps you pinpoint your practice's diagnosis at any given time. My own business was operating in a higher level when I boarded the plane to New Jersey, but when the pandemic hit, it went right back down to the focus on **SALES**. This tool is not meant to assess your stage of growth or tell you how well you're doing. Any business can have an unmet need at any time, in any level.

I beg of you, please don't get lost in the levels. They are only a point of reference, a checkpoint on your journey. As long as you understand and can recite in your sleep that the goal of your business is profitability and the purpose of your business is your *why*, you will be fine. In fact, you will be more than fine. You will be awesome! Everything you're going to learn in each of the levels will help you support both your goal and your purpose. I wouldn't be able to live with myself if I couldn't promise that to you.

MAKE AN IMPACT AND LEAVE A LEGACY

Reader, there's something I want to tell you. If you're familiar with the first *Fix This Next*, you will see something quite different in this book. In this one, written specifically for you, there are two things you will not find that were in the original. While the levels of **IMPACT** and **LEGACY** are extremely important, you won't see chapters dedicated to them here. Instead, you will find them woven throughout every chapter and every page, present in every word. I tie it all together for you in the last section of the book, "You Can and You Will," so make sure you read that when you get to the end.

I chose to focus on **SALES**, **PROFIT**, and **ORDER** because that's where I can help you most. It's important to me that I make sure you are able to use the HHN to make a proper business diagnosis. You know from years of treating patients that if you apply a treatment plan to the wrong diagnosis, the treatment just won't work—no matter how good it is.

HOW THE HHN WORKS

Imagine you are a plumber. I know, I know, just humor me! You pull up to a job in your new truck with its fancy built-in toolbox in the back. Your tool belt is firmly secured around your waist and you're ready to face whatever the kitchen sink is about to give you. You assess the situation. You triage that baby. You give it a good once-over, pour some colored liquid down the drain, and look to see if the goop is coming out of the pipe, like it should, or if it's coming out somewhere it shouldn't. You watch closely, looking for anything that appears out of the norm.

While you wait, you test the hot and cold handles and look for rust. Then you check your clog again. You whip out your long metal testy thing with a meter on the end that tells you how bad the clog actually is. The last thing you want to do is waste your time fixing the wrong thing. Wait! There it is. You see it. The culprit. It's square, appears to be covered in little raised bumps, and you think, squinting one eye and closing the other, that it kinda looks red. Wait, it's recognizable. It's a Lego! Your hand instinctually reaches for the tool you know will get the job done.

There are many parallels between the ways you provide clinical services, operate your business, and unclog a sink. Your business has problems, and it needs you to assess it objectively. It needs you to be the confident one, the one who pulls the HHN from your toolbox and asks what matters most. In order to get the right answer, you must ask the right questions. Then, and only then, you can create a treatment plan to take your business from ordinary to extraordinary.

When you are confident in your business's most impactful need, you can be sure that no effort goes to waste. Using the HHN is the best way to ensure that you're always on the right path toward your goal. At the lowest level HHN, you will find **SALES**. Ask yourself the five questions found in this level, starting with number one. If you answer no to any of the questions, congratulations, you have just identified a Core Need. Just to forewarn you, there's a good chance you will answer no to more than one question. If so, that's okay. It just means you have to conduct a *differential diagnosis*. The great thing about the HHN is that it will do this for you. The corresponding numbers will tell you the order in which to address the diagnoses, with the lowest number always taking precedence.

You are looking for an unmet Core Need at the lowest foundational level. Once you have landed on this Core Need, you move on to step two and apply the diagnosis. This should be "fixed next" because more often than not, satisfying this problem corrects so many others automatically.

RECAP: Steps to Diagnose Your Practice

1. Answer yes or no to all the questions on the HHN, starting with the **SALES** level.
2. Circle every NO.
3. Star the NO with the lowest number on the lowest foundational level.

That's your diagnosis!

Let's try it together! Tara is a practice owner in Missouri and has a crazy love for couples' counseling. When Tara used the HHN as a diagnostic tool for her practice, she answered no on Prospect Attraction (2) and Client Conversion (3). These would both be deemed unmet Core Needs. Since Prospect Attraction (2) has an associated number lower than that of Client Conversion (3), Prospect Attraction is her practice's diagnosis. This means that all of Tara's efforts should be focused on treating this diagnosis.

Let's say Tara is an incredibly creative marketing genius and decided to create a buzz in her community by painting rocks with the hashtag #counselinghubrocks. As it turns out, this was so successful that she met her unmet need of Prospect Attraction.

Now she comes back to the HHN, ready to reassess. This time, her previous unmet need is now satisfied, but Client Conversion is still unmet. It is now the only unmet need in her foundational level of **SALES**. So, what is her diagnosis?

Yes, it's Client Conversion. While she quickly satisfied her first unmet need, she still needs to employ interventions to convert the new leads coming in from the painted rocks strategy!

Can you see how Tara identified her Core Needs, chose the lowest unmet need on the numerical scale, labeled it as her diagnosis, and focused her attention on treating it? After successful treatment, she reassessed and determined that the only unmet need left was Client Conversion. That became her diagnosis, and she will treat it accordingly.

INTERPRETING THE RESULTS

If you're honest with yourself as you assess your practice, you might be shocked by the results of your HHN assessment. When you really think about the questions asked in each foundational level and strive to answer them thoughtfully, issues you knew were there but just never paid much attention to may come to the surface. As you land on a diagnosis, the unmet Core Need at the lowest level, it's important to collect as much data as you possibly can to support it. This is called *baseline data,* and it will help you develop a treatment that will support the goal and serve the purpose.

Let's assume that, as much as you'd love to avoid this painful realization, you have identified a diagnosis of Collecting on Commitments. It's important to gather baseline data, which in this case might be the status of your accounts receivable report or anecdotal data from your biller. You basically need to find out why on God's green earth you're not being paid for the claims you have submitted. Are they going out the same day, or is there a lag for some reason? Gathering this critical information will set you up for a strong and well-developed treatment plan.

Looking at financial reports is like looking at the dashboard of a car. Although I most certainly don't know how to fix anything under the hood, I can definitely tell when there's a problem because of the little warning lights on the dashboard. I'm a clinician, not a biller or a mechanic. I know just enough to get myself in trouble, and just enough to know when I have a problem. Fortunately, that's really all I need to know. With a financial system showcasing clear green, yellow, and red indicators, I have enough information to take to my billing department and say, "Hey, what's going on with our claims?" Then they can do the work under the hood.

When you're equipped with the data to support your practice's diagnosis, you can get to a solution much more quickly and effectively. So, when you assess your practice, I encourage you to look for informational gaps and create or pull together tools that will help provide the information you need to fully understand the problem.

With a diagnosis in hand, you can start the process of treating your practice. You know as well as I that it all starts with the right diagnosis. From there you can develop goals, interventions, and a plan to evaluate progress. A treatment plan for your practice is no different than a treatment plan for your clients. It gives them a sense of direction, and you the confidence that you're moving closer to your goal, further in pursuit of your purpose.

At this point, I want you to think about *your* purpose—or, as author Simon Sinek would say, your "why."[4] Although the goal of our businesses is always profitability, your purpose belongs entirely to *you*. Your purpose is *why* you started and *why* you keep pushing even when things are tough. It's the reason you begin each morning with a fresh cup of coffee and let go of all the frustrations of the day before.

It's the child who is overlooked by everyone else, but lights up because they know you *see* them. It's the longtime client who, one day out of the blue, turns around and thanks you for everything you did that *one time*. It's that adult who smiles confidently as they pass you in the grocery section of your local Walmart, and now only bears the slightest resemblance to the misguided teen you mentored all through high school.

---

[4] Simon Sinek, *Start With Why: How Great Leaders Inspire Everyone to Take Action* (London: Penguin Business, 2011).

Start with the Goal and Finish with Purpose

The goal of our business is profitability, forever and always. Everything you do from this point forward, whether it's making the diagnosis, creating interventions, or reassessing, will be with the goal in mind. It's profitability that provides the opportunity to live out the purpose for which we started, and never to forget the purpose for which we continue.

> Reader, what is your purpose? Write it down. Plaster it all over your office. Place it where you can see it; position it so it can't help but inform everything you do. When times are tough and problems are hard, you'll revisit your purpose and it will keep you going. Most importantly, pursue that purpose with every ounce of your being. Then, it will all be worth it.

Chapter Three

Without SALES, Nothing Else Matters

Every Saturday morning at the crack of dawn, I'd prepare my kitchen in the little loft apartment I rented above a deli downtown. Flour, eggs, milk. Check! Vegetable oil, powdered sugar, and honey. Check! Apron on, music playing, Kitchen-Aid mixer prepped, and I was ready for a day of cupcakes. Honey beehive cupcakes, to be exact. These delicious little gems would be my ticket to lots of moolah, and all the other prestigious things I imagined came along with being an entrepreneur.

I had daydreamed about it since my early twenties: I would own my own business, and my life would be packed full of long vacations and loads of confidence. Money would pour in so fast I wouldn't even know how to spend it. I'd have nice cars, a closet full of designer clothes, and a big, beautiful house that looked as though it was straight out of *Lifestyles of the Rich and Famous*.

I'd lie in bed at night and think about how entrepreneurs must be super smart, maybe even geniuses. (After all, you can't own a business if you aren't, right?) Checking the mail would be fun. Cascades of expensive envelopes, stuffed with the fancy party invitations that only VIP bank customers get, would fall out each time I opened the mailbox lid. As an entrepreneur, I would be sought out to serve as a board member for nearly every organization in town. And when I walked into a room, I would stand proud and no longer feel invisible.

Before I knew it, my twenties became my thirties, and I gave in. I dabbled in business. This is when I began baking those cute little honey-pot cupcakes. The problem was that, despite my enthusiasm, my work never brought me a glamorous lifestyle. I had fun and kept myself busy, but I was not asked to be on any board, I was not rolling in the dough, and I was definitely not being recognized for my contribution to our local economy. The most shocking part of all was, when I walked into a room, I still felt invisible. What was I doing wrong?

I didn't commit to my business or to myself. I had sales, but I couldn't tell you how much. I sold what I had, when I had it. I didn't track my overhead, my profit margins, or my return on investment (ROI). I made knee-jerk decisions about what to sell, when to sell it, and who to sell it to. I used a reactionary approach to business; I just sat back and waited for sales to happen. "If you build it, they will come," said the voice in the field from the movie *Field of Dreams.*

Not true in my case. I built lots of things and no one ever came. I expected customers to line up around the corner to buy my cupcakes, but they didn't. Posting those cute attention-getting images on social media brought traffic my way, but not enough. When someone commented and my notifications pinged, it was like I hit the jackpot!

"Cha-ching! I just made $28!" Whenever I made a sale, I was stoked. After all, that's the point, right? To sell things? *Wrong.* I had missed one step of the many I didn't yet know existed.

That $28 didn't get me far. In fact, it barely covered my overhead expenses. It didn't even cover payment for my time at minimum wage. What was once an entrepreneurial fantasy soon became my unforgiving reality. I packed up my mixer, boxed up my supplies, and shut down my cupcake business. I had learned my lesson.

Making sales is about so much more than getting someone to buy something. It's about selling in a deliberate way, with the goal of profitability at the forefront. It's about meeting your own personal lifestyle needs while attracting the right people to your service and convincing them to book an appointment with you instead of the place across the street. It's about doing all the things you say you will do. It's about the transfer of funds from the consumer to you, the seller, that aligns with your business's expectations.

It took several more years, after the brilliant but delusional cupcake fantasy, for me to see that sales weren't going to happen *to* me or *for* me. They were going to happen *by* me, and that meant taking a hard look at my goal and the five Core Needs that had to be fulfilled in order to get me there. For us as healthcare professionals, making a sale means serving a client—taking care of their needs to achieve wellness. Your business will never take care of itself. It needs you or your employees to tend to it, assess its issues, and implement interventions for improvement. It needs you to give it a treatment plan.

After working with thousands of clients in the last several years, it has become crystal clear to me that business owners pull their sales goals straight out of their behinds. They hear their buddy's goal, and they increase theirs by 20% just to have the edge. They look for industry standards and base their goals on something that may or may not have any similarities to their own business when, in reality, they should base their sales goals on their practice, their needs, and their desires—not on Sally Sue with a cool logo and a mega-practice on the hill.

These random goals we create stem from random people with random benchmarks. Don't look outside to figure out what your practice should be working toward on the inside; just look within, to yourself. What do you need in order to have the lifestyle *you* desire? That's all that matters. What others think about sales is not important right now. These are the same people who believe sales is about getting people to buy things, but it isn't. Sales is the bloodline, the lifeline, the creation of cash for your practice. You must treat it with the utmost importance and give it the respect it deserves. You do that by satisfying all of its needs before looking to another level.

SALES IS A RELATIONSHIP

Whether cupcakes or counseling services, I have always sold my product to a consumer: someone who recognizes that they either need something or want something. Back then, my little business had an opportunity to convince customers to buy from me through a conversation, a pricing strategy, or—best-case scenario—a product that spoke for itself.

When the consumer chooses us, we enter into a committed relationship with them and will nurture and grow it for as long as we possibly can. Your relationship with your clients can be understood in five distinct stages:

1. **The Connection:** This is the first part of the sales process, but you may think of it as what happens before the sale. In order for you to get clients to consider buying from you, you first have to make them aware that you exist, then help them see that you have the services and skills that will help fulfill a need they have. If you are not authentic, consistent, and deliberate in your marketing, you may end up with clients you have no business serving, and that means things can go wonky even before you "get the sale." The Connection phase is the sale before the sale.

2. **The Agreement:** The agreement states the terms of the sale. In our industry, we're talking about client consent forms and fee agreements.

3. **The Deliverable:** This is when the provider completes the service promised to the client as outlined in the agreement and the client's treatment plan. This is when you do what you say you're going to do.

4. **The Collection:** In this stage, the client pays you for the service you provide within the time parameters outlined in your consent form and fee agreement. (Cha-ching!)

5. **The Conclusion:** This is when all agreed-upon terms are delivered and both parties confirm that everything is complete. This might look like successful completion of treatment goals, a parenting program, or a set of fillings for all those cavities! This may also be when the client decides to continue with additional treatment and new terms are stated.

As the seller, you make a commitment when you accept a form of payment in return for a service. This is more than just an exchange of money. It's about clarifying a message, generating a buzz, and delivering and collecting on your commitments. And it's about doing these things so well that you satisfy your client in a way that leaves them feeling better than they did when they started.

As the consumer, the client makes a commitment to you in much the same way. When they seek out your services and agree to your terms, you better make for dang sure they come through, because otherwise things could go south, quickly.

A fellow practice owner here in my home state, whom we'll call Tina, experienced a wave of sales in her outpatient medication management treatment practice. With a shortage of providers in her area and a massive need for medication assistance, her practice exploded. It was basically full on day one. So many new clients, so many billable claims—this was going to be so good!

In order to keep up with the demand, Tina hired as many providers she could. And before she knew it, her little dream of owning a business became a reality. It was happening, and no matter how hard she tried, there never seemed to be enough providers to keep up with the constant client inquiries. She was pulled in a million different directions, her dopamine levels were through the roof, and she was pumped. It was all she could do to get through each day without any disasters while eagerly waiting for that money to start rolling in.

But it never came. Tina was so consumed with the number of new leads, all the claims to file, and all the providers she needed to hire that she neglected to pay attention to actually getting paid. Her biller was unable to keep up with the demand, so incorrect claims were going out, and that meant lots of denials. To save time, the practice didn't collect payments up front and instead billed clients after they received services. Disaster. Big freaking catastrophe. Those clients that had so desperately needed Tina's help wouldn't pay her.

All of this stress, coupled with the increased overhead from the slew of providers she had hired, pushed Tina over the edge. She had to threaten clients with collection agencies, fire her biller, and tell all the providers she'd hired that she couldn't afford to pay them anymore. She became infected by analysis paralysis and couldn't move forward—or backward, for that matter. Tina lost tons of time and loads of money, and, even worse, she tarnished her relationship with the community.

This is quite an extreme cautionary tale, but it really happened to Tina and it happens to entrepreneurs all the time. We lose sight of our business's Core Needs, and when that happens in the foundational level of **SALES**, things can turn terrible, fast. As healthcare professionals, I realize it doesn't always *feel* good for us to associate the term "sales" with our business. It may feel sleazy or slimy. We certainly don't think of selling as a foundational need for our practice's success. Like it or not, despite our industry, **SALES** is in fact the core level of our practice.

Now, let's go over the five Core Needs your company must meet in order to stabilize your **SALES** level on the HHN so you don't end up like Tina.

SALES LEVEL

1 **Lifestyle Congruence**
Do you know what your billable sessions/services must be in order to support your personal financial comfort level?

2 **Prospect and Provider Attraction**
Do you attract enough clients to support your level of needed sales for a profitable practice (20% net profit or higher), and do you attract enough providers to support the patient demand?

3 **Client Conversion**
Do you convert enough of the right clients to support your level of needed billable sessions/services?

4 **Delivering on Commitments**
Do you fully deliver to your clients by doing what your message promises, following through, and ultimately meeting your clients' health goals?

5 **Collecting on Commitments**
Do your clients fully deliver on their commitment to you to attend sessions as scheduled, with minimal no-shows and late cancelations? Do they pay promptly for your services?

DIAGNOSIS #1:
Lifestyle Congruence

Question: *Do you know what your practice's sales (billable sessions) must be in order to support your personal financial comfort level?*

Presenting Problem/Symptoms: Have you ever felt like you were wingin' it? Like back in those college days, when you weren't super clear on how many classes you had to show up for, how many homework assignments you needed to turn in, and how many tests you had to make at least a C on in order to pass? Lifestyle Congruence in business is similar to this.

Most business owners show up to work and do the best they can, but don't have a clear-cut goal to work toward in order to pay their bills and live the life they want to live. If this sounds familiar, you could be feeling a sense of confusion, uncertainty, or doubt. You may even feel like your business's numbers are a mystery. You know they're there, but you're not sure how to interpret them. You may feel inadequate when someone asks you the question, "Do you know how many billable sessions per week your practice must have in order to support your personal financial comfort level?"

If you can relate, it's okay. Many of us don't realize our own Lifestyle Congruence. We don't know the number of services our practice must produce in order for us to pay our mortgage, make the car payment, and afford all of our monthly necessities. The fact of the matter is, when you have a clear Lifestyle Congruence number, you're exponentially more likely to achieve it. There's a simple formula for determining this metric, which we talk more about in FTN QuickStart. But for right now, here are some examples of possible interventions.

Possible Interventions: In order to determine Lifestyle Congruence (LC), you need to know: How much money do you need to make, in a year, to live the life you want? Once you have this number, take your LC number and divide it by your average reimbursement for the service you provide. This will tell you how many of those sessions your practice must complete in one year to meet your goal. Divide that number by 12 to determine how many services it will be necessary to complete in one month to stay on track. This is going to vary a little depending on how you pay yourself, but you will get an idea of what your practice's financial goals need to be in order to achieve your Lifestyle Congruence.

$$\frac{\text{LIFESTYLE CONGRUENCE}}{\text{AVERAGE REIMBURSEMENT}} = \text{SESSIONS NEEDED PER YEAR}$$

$$\frac{\text{SESSIONS NEEDED PER YEAR}}{\text{12 MONTHS}} = \text{SESSIONS NEEDED PER MONTH}$$

Lifestyle Congruence sometimes means more than just the numbers. It can mean taking a good hard look at the life you are living now versus the lifestyle you desire. In some situations, it will mean editing: cutting out the costs that provide little to no value, the things you continue to pay for even though you rarely use them. It's not about sacrifice, necessarily; it's about making necessary adjustments to live the life you want.

Example: Sara is a mental health group practice owner who has worked hard to get as many new clients as possible into her new practice. She has been extremely focused on sales and is starting to feel overwhelmed and a little burned out. She's not sure if she's doing the right things, or if it is even possible to scale back at this point.

She knows her goal is to personally make at least $100,000 per year, starting in the upcoming year. At this time, she pays herself 20% of the company's gross revenue as an owner's salary. In these circumstances, she needs to gross $500,000 in order to meet her Lifestyle Congruence since $100,000 is 20% of $500,000. To take it one step further, Sara's average reimbursement rate for the services she provides is $100. She takes the $500,000 goal and divides it by 100, which tells her she must produce 5,000 sessions per year and 417 sessions per month.

GOAL: $100,000 PER YEAR

SALARY: 20% OF GROSS

$$\frac{\$100,000}{20\%} = \$500,000 \text{ PER YEAR}$$

TREATMENT PLAN:
Lifestyle Congruence

1. **Presenting Problem:** Sara feels overwhelmed and has started to get burned out. She's unclear on her practice's numbers, and she doesn't know how many billable sessions she needs to meet her personal Lifestyle Congruence.

2. **Diagnosis:** Lifestyle Congruence

3. **Strengths:** Sara is great with organization and pays attention to detail. She also has a waiting list of clients who want to be seen at her practice.

4. **Baseline:** Sara has determined that she needs to personally make $8,333 per month ($100,000 annually) in order to pay her bills

and cover all her household expenses. Since she uses the Profit First model, her accountant recommended that she allocate 20% of gross revenue for owner's compensation. (Everyone's compensation structure is different, so please, just focus on yours for now.) Sara needs to figure out how much gross revenue the practice must generate in order for her 20% allocation to equal $100,000 annually.

5. **Goal:** Sara will determine the number of billable sessions her practice must produce in order to meet her Lifestyle Congruence of $8,333 per month. That way, she can create a plan to achieve that number of sessions.

6. **Interventions:**

   1. Sara will use the billable session formula to determine all the components necessary to reach the goal.

   $$\frac{\text{AMOUNT OF SALARY}}{\text{PERCENTAGE OF SALARY}} = \text{PRACTICE'S GROSS}$$

   2. She will divide the total gross by 12 months to get the monthly gross revenue needed.

   $$\frac{\text{GROSS REVENUE}}{12} = \text{MONTHLY REVENUE}$$

   3. She will divide the monthly total by the average service reimbursement rate to get the total number of sessions per month.

   $$\frac{\text{MONTHLY REVENUE}}{\text{REIMBURSEMENT RATE}} = \text{TOTAL SESSIONS NEEDED PER MONTH}$$

4. She will divide the total number of sessions per month by four weeks (actually, the average number of weeks per month is 4.33) to get the total number of sessions per week needed to reach her goal.

$$\frac{\text{SESSIONS NEEDED PER MONTH}}{4.33} = \text{TOTAL SESSIONS NEEDED PER WEEK}$$

5. She will create a dashboard (spreadsheet) to track weekly sessions or use the capabilities of her Electronic Health Records system to ensure that she meets her milestones and achieves her goal.

7. **Plan for Progress:** Sara will check the dashboard weekly to evaluate progress and ensure the number of sessions needed are being performed. After the first month of tracking, she will reevaluate her Lifestyle Congruence to make sure it is still accurate and nothing needs to be adjusted.

DIAGNOSIS #2:
Prospect and Provider Attraction

Question: *Do you attract enough clients to support your level of needed sales for a profitable practice (20% net or higher is industry standard), and do you attract enough providers to support the patient demand?*

Presenting Symptoms: I hear this diagnosis in one of two ways: A practice has more providers than patients or more patients than providers. This is a dangerous dichotomy and hard to remedy. Symptoms of this Core Need include having more clients than you can serve; a waiting list that is taking on a life of its own; provider turnover, which results in more patients on your waiting list; or, even worse, patients who leave to follow the lost provider.

Perhaps you hired your support staff on projected productivity metrics. You designed your budget to include two receptionists, a biller, and an office manager, but your billable sessions have decreased so much that you're finding it hard to make payroll. Have your phones slowed down or, worse, stopped altogether? Maybe you have an all-self-pay practice and, given the circumstances of today's world, people are opting to use their insurance benefits. You might feel like you must work *way too hard* to make *not enough money*. If this sounds like you, you might have a Prospect or Provider Attraction diagnosis.

Possible Interventions for Provider Attraction: Cathy struggled to balance providers with prospects. It seemed like she always had more of one and less of the other. This made it difficult to make long-term decisions for her practice. She was in a highly competitive market and it was difficult to stand out. Cathy created a highly niched, unique service within her practice. Since no other providers in her area were offering this service, she knew that finding the right, experienced provider to hire for the position would be nearly impossible. So Cathy built a unique training program into her practice that eliminated all of her competition. Her practice became *the* one for court-ordered therapy and high-risk cases. It worked! She started to attract the right types of providers, ones that were invested in her mission and had every reason to stay for the long haul.

Possible Interventions for Prospect Attraction: In the same way Cathy used her new program to attract prospects and train them according to her model, she used its momentum and buzz to spark excitement in her community. She began marketing her new service and, before she knew it, it took off! She designed a marketing campaign for all the community partners who would be potential referral sources and started to speak their language in email and print campaigns. Professionals in her community heard her message and started to listen. Since hers was the only business providing this service, all referrals came to her!

TREATMENT PLAN:
Prospect Attraction

1. **Presenting Problem:** Cathy is having trouble getting enough clients into her practice to fill her current providers' schedules.

2. **Diagnosis:** Prospect Attraction

3. **Strengths:** Cathy has a reliable system for tracking phone calls and leads from her website and Google ads.

4. **Baseline:** Cathy currently receives between one and two calls per day, which is not enough to fill her providers' schedules.

5. **Goal:** Cathy will receive five new inquiries per day for the next 30 days.

6. **Interventions:**

   1. Cathy will examine the sources of her current leads and make direct and deliberate contact with those referral sources, informing them about the availability of the new providers in her practice. She will utilize her strength in tracking leads to examine this information properly and minimize any wasted effort.

2. She will look for barriers in her community and create a strategy to tap into them with targeted messaging. She already has a good relationship with the legal community, so she will start there.

7. **Plan for Progress:** Cathy will note the start date of these interventions in her dashboard, which tracks all new leads. She will monitor the progress weekly to determine what strategy is most effective. Once she is able to isolate the most effective approach, she will increase its intensity to reach more community partners and obtain more referrals.

DIAGNOSIS #3:
Client Conversion

Question: *Do you convert enough of the right clients to support your level of needed sales?*

Depending on the type of practice you have, Client Conversion could be a big issue or a non-issue. Conversion is taking a lead and converting it into a billable session for your practice—essentially, a sale. If you have a fee-for-service practice, only accept out-of-network benefits, or take limited types of insurance, this is the lifeline for your practice. Although many people are willing and able to forgo their insurance altogether, the majority will use it if they're paying an out-of-pocket fee each pay period. I never have a shortage of questions on this topic. People want a magic script, a foolproof unicorn, when it comes to converting leads into patients. Unfortunately, you must find a system that is both authentic to your business and works for your ideal client and target market, and that's often through trial and error.

Presenting Symptoms: Like so many clients I have worked with, you have a couple of problems. Your conversion rate is low, *but* you get a ton of leads. The phone rings off the hook, but when clients find out yours is a self-pay practice, they end the call immediately. You understand their position, but this makes your conversion percentage seem low. Perhaps, given your low conversion rate, you've considered modifying your model and starting to accept more kinds of insurance. After all, you're willing to put up with the hassle if it gets more people in the door.

If you're a practice that has no issue with conversion because you've committed to a deal with the devil (insurance—just kidding, sorta), you'll likely skip this Core Need but acquire a Collecting on Commitments diagnosis. Our needs will often change based on our practice model, and this one tends to be pretty common. Where you manage to forgo some problems (insurance) for more clients, you will be forced to trade volume for a potential Prospect Attraction problem. There's no right or wrong way to approach this; it's all about what you prefer to battle: fighting with insurance companies or attracting new clients.

Possible Interventions: You must start by being confident in the transformational services your practice offers. Be clear on your message, and be able to communicate it clearly to all leads through all platforms. In his book *Lingo,* Jeffrey Shaw talks about the importance of speaking the client's language and making sure that your words match up with their needs.[5] For you, this could be a script that you've tried and tested, or it could be ensuring that your website's headline and subtitle speak directly to your ideal client.

---

[5] Jeffrey Shaw, *Lingo: Discover Your Ideal Customer's Secret Language and Make Your Business Irresistible* (Miami Beach, FL: Creative Warriors Press, 2018).

This could also mean reevaluating your client avatar. It's likely you need to focus more specifically on the clients you're trying to attract, speaking directly to them rather than trying to cast a wide net. Many of my former consulting clients have found success in inventorying their current patients, paying attention to the language they use to describe their needs, and speaking directly to those stated needs with their marketing message. You could ask what is most important to them in the services they seek, and offer that. Oftentimes, conversions are unsuccessful because we try to convert the wrong clients to satisfy our need for sales. When we target the right clients for our practice, speak their language and become intentional in our approach, our conversion rate will increase.

TREATMENT PLAN:
Client Conversion

1. **Presenting Problem:** Jessica owns a self-pay practice and struggles to convert this type of client. In her community, the majority of other practices are insurance-based, and her leads are not used to the fee-for-service concept.

2. **Diagnosis:** Client Conversion

3. **Baseline:** Jessica receives approximately 10 new calls per week, and converts an average of one client per week. This means her conversion rate is 10%.

4. **Strengths:** Jessica is strongly connected to online communities such as The Private Practice Startup,[6] where she can get paperwork packets and scripts for easily converting self-pay clients.

---

[6] The Private Practice Startup: Check out Kate and Katie's amazing Facebook group and tell them Kasey sent you!

5. **Goal:** Within the next 30 days, Jessica's practice will increase its conversion rate from 10% to 50% in order to support its sales goals.

6. **Interventions:**

   1. Jessica will examine her current script for converting clients, looking for points in the conversation where clients tend to back out of the process. She will rework the flow of the script so that clients understand what they have to lose if they do not engage in the specific type of therapy she offers, and with her practice.

   2. During this process, she will evaluate what differentiates her practice and ensure that those features are clearly outlined in the script. She will also make sure they are prominently displayed on her website and all social media platforms.

7. **Plan for Progress:** With reworked script in hand, Jessica will track calls daily, looking for data to help inform her next round of interventions. She is aware that it will take several modifications before she achieves the conversion percentage she is shooting for, so all the information she can get will help. If the conversion percentage is not improved by modifying the script alone, her next step will be to target her audience more specifically and narrow the sales funnel.

DIAGNOSIS #4:
Delivering on Commitments

Question: *Do you fully deliver on your commitments to your clients?*

This is where you ask yourself, can I put my money where my mouth is? In other words, does my marketing message line up with my actions? If I promise all new clients will be seen within 48 hours, is that actually happening? If my brand promise is "A place where people feel cared for," do I have systems and processes in place to ensure that clients do feel cared for at all junctions along their journey with my practice? If I advertise a pain-free dental experience, is that really happening?

If not, you have not delivered on your commitments, and your patients know it.

Presenting Symptoms: Symptoms of this Core Need includes patients bold enough to say, "That's false advertising!" You know the ones I'm talking about—the ones who love to take to social media to express their frustrations. They blast you on Facebook for not being the miracle worker you claim to be. Although *you* know they didn't follow through with any of the recommendations you gave them, the world doesn't, and now you look like a jerk.

Let's say that one of your providers, who carried a massive caseload, has left your practice. You haven't been able to bring on a new provider fast enough, and now you can no longer live up to your promise to schedule your new clients for appointments within 48 hours. Guess what? You have failed to deliver on your commitments.

See how simple it is for our commitments to get the best of us? We have good intentions, but they don't always work out. This Core Need is a great reality check for us. We must ensure that all of our messaging is truthful, and that we can back it up without any uncertainty.

Possible Interventions: Start by making a list of all the commitments you make to your patients, including everything from session wait time to the clinical improvements they will experience. Assess yourself in your practice's delivery. Whatever you identify as an unmet commitment will require a treatment plan to change its status. It's better and more realistic to promise less than to under-deliver on all your promises just to get people in the door, so assess the reasons you're unable to deliver on the commitments and put a plan in place to address those instead. Many practices don't take the time they need to manage their patients' expectations. This could manifest in a lack of informed consent, missing or confusing fine print, or questions that are not clearly answered prior to the start of treatment. If so, there must be a plan in place to remedy the situation so that your clients have clearly managed expectations.

TREATMENT PLAN:
Delivering on Commitments

1. **Presenting Problem:** Counseling Collective has become known in their community for scheduling new patients within 72 hours. They have been slammed with new referrals and now have a waiting list.

2. **Diagnosis:** Delivering on Commitments

3. **Baseline:** Counseling Collective promises referral sources a 72-hour turnaround time on new referrals, but they now have 44 people on their waiting list and it doesn't look like there will be an opening for at least a month.

4. **Strengths:** The practice has an amazing client care coordinator (CCC) who is able to explain this to clients and referral sources without them getting too upset.

5. **Goal:** The CCC will reduce the waiting list to zero so that the practice can honor its commitment to a 72-hour turnaround time for new clients.

6. **Interventions:**
   1. The CCC will triage the client care system to make sure the data is accurate.
   2. The CCC will reach out to all clinicians and ask if they are available to take any new clients to clear the waiting list.
   3. The CCC will choose one clinician and ask them to block off time for initial sessions only. This clinician can book clients on the waiting list for intake appointments, then assign them to another provider who has an expected opening within the next two to four weeks.
   4. All clients who are inactive or have more than one no-show will be removed from the clinician's client list, and someone from the waiting list will be booked in their place.

7. **Plan for Progress:** Based on these interventions, Counseling Collective's waiting list should be cleared within one week. The human resources director will begin hiring new providers immediately so that the practice is not in this position again.

DIAGNOSIS #5:
Collecting on Commitments

Question: *Do your clients fully deliver on their commitments to you?*

When you accept a new client in your practice, you enter into a mutual agreement. You will provide a service and they will pay you. Simple, right? Wrong. Let me be clear, there are good, honest, dependable people out there in this world. Still, in my years in practice, I have been utterly shocked at the number of clients who don't pay their balances. The highest percentage of people with open invoices are those who are more than capable of paying on time and paying in full.

Recently, I went to a new dentist's office where I chose to use out-of-network benefits for the procedures I needed. After the exam and diagnosis, I was presented with a treatment plan outlining all of the procedures and their associated costs. It was made extremely clear that I would be required to pay up front for the service, but the office would submit the bill to my insurance and I would then receive a check from the insurance company. It was also made clear to me that the dentist's office could not guarantee that my insurance would pay anything. This is a perfect example of managing a patient's expectations. Now, if my insurance decides to not pay my bill, I might be upset, but not with the dental practice.

Presenting Symptoms: If yours is an insurance-based practice and Collecting on Commitments is your diagnosis, you will see a high accounts receivable balance. Your number of outstanding claims grows week after week, month after month. Out of the 852 reasons an insurance company can deny your claim, you experience a variety of them with each of the patients you have seen but not been paid for. Maybe your claims are denied due to a taxonomy issue, maybe the wrong NPI was listed, or perhaps there's a problem on the payer's side. Regardless of the reason, you haven't been paid though you've done the work. There could be many more reasons for this, all of which we'll talk more about in the Interventions chapter; nonetheless, you have done the work and you're not being paid. Maybe you own a self-pay practice, but don't require your clients to pay up front. They conveniently forgot their wallet, need to write you a check, or will call in an hour later to pay you for the work you did. But guess what? They never do. They made a commitment to you and you are unable to collect on it.

Possible Interventions: Manage your clients' expectations. You have policies for many reasons, and this is just one of them. Revisit your policy for collecting on payments and make modifications as needed. Many practices are moving to the pay-at-time-of-booking model, which eliminates collection problems. I use this model in my consulting business, and I would never stray from it. What you think might be doing clients a favor—not making them pay up front or at the time of service—may actually be a hindrance to them. They may have the money now, but might not in a month (or whenever you get around to sending out the statement).

TREATMENT PLAN:
Collecting on Commitments

1. **Presenting Problem:** Precision Dental has never required its clients to keep a credit card on file. Co-payments have always been collected at time of visit, and any remaining balance after insurance pays the practice on behalf of the client is then billed to

the client separately. Clients aren't paying their invoices, and the practice is spending a ton of money on postage and wasting too much time calling clients about their bills.

2. **Diagnosis:** Collecting on Commitments

3. **Baseline:** The practice has $2,589 in outstanding patient balances as a result of unpaid co-pays and outstanding insurance payments.

4. **Strengths:** The practice has a biller who is very persistent and understands systems and processes well.

5. **Goal:** The practice will reduce its patient balances by 90% in the next 45 days.

6. **Interventions:**

   1. The current consents and fee schedule will need to be updated immediately. The updated materials will state that the practice requires a credit card on file for each patient, and that any outstanding balances will be charged immediately.

   2. This new policy will be sent out to all patients within five business days. It will also be communicated with the providers, so they can talk about it with their patients.

   3. The billing department will get payment information from patients immediately, and systems will be developed around when to charge patients for payments.

   4. As the billing department contacts patients to obtain this information, it will charge their cards for any outstanding balances.

   5. The company will update their payment policy to reflect that payment in full must be collected at time of

session should there be any question about the amount of coverage. In the event a client's insurance pays, the client will be refunded immediately.

7. **Plan for Progress:** The practice manager will evaluate this timeline weekly. If the balance has not decreased by 90% in 45 days, she will assess the situation and determine likely causes. Then she will put additional interventions in place to prevent this from happening in the future.

ALWAYS START WITH SALES

When you have clarity around how much is needed to support your lifestyle, setting sales goals becomes easy. It's the first Core Need I share with you for a reason; without this understanding, your business will be built from someone else's random goal, not your own intentional one. Since it's the first need within the first level, it's sure to be important! (Note that, while you always start at the bottom level of the HHN and work your way up, you don't have to work through the Core Needs in sequence *within* that level.)

In the foundational level of **SALES**, we begin to realize that the entrepreneurial fantasies we once had were more like delusions, and the belief that our lives were destined for fame and fortune was just a fictional scenario we conjured up in our minds. We understand that reality is more closely aligned with late nights, wild gray hairs, and frown lines, and have gone from wishing we were no longer invisible to hoping to goodness no one sees us in public. We start to see that running a business is different than we had expected. It requires an actual strategy. Instead of the "build it and they will come" philosophy we heard when we were starting out, it's now the "build it and then you're done" philosophy. We're tired, it's hard, and we may not yet realize that there's more to it than selling just to sell.

The HHN helped me see what I had been missing all along. I saw how gaining clarity about what I needed to support my lifestyle would help my business move in the right direction. That's why Lifestyle Congruence is the first Core Need in the first foundational level. It's the framework from which all else is built. **SALES** is at the base of the HHN because without it, nothing else matters. Without sales, there can be no profit. Without profit, there's no point in creating order—which ultimately allows you to system-ize and scale.

Without **SALES**, **PROFIT**, and **ORDER**, it is impossible to create life-long **IMPACT** and **LEGACY**. This is where I see business owners who are in it for all the right reasons, but are missing the point of sales. They rely on their purpose and their purpose alone to keep the doors open, and it's just not enough. Good intentions will not make you money; sales will.

In the next chapter, I'll share more about the mindset shift Cathy experienced when she locked onto the HHN framework. Hang tight, it's a good one!

Chapter Four

Achieve PROFIT on Purpose

"Can I—?" she began in a very soft whisper.

"No way!" I said. I cut her off a little more abruptly than I meant to. I wasn't trying to be rude; I'm just very passionate about this subject.

"But it's her three-month anniversary, so could I maybe—?" she tried again, with a little more conviction.

"Nope!" I piped up before she even had the chance to say it. I knew what was about to come out of that mouth.

"But she's so bubbly!" she exclaimed. This was a last ditch-effort to convince me that her brand-new employee, the one she was already overpaying, deserved a raise and an anniversary present because she had successfully made it three months into her employment.

"I know you love your team (she won't let me call them employees), but you can't until you become profitable. If there's nothing to give, where are you going to get it from?"

Cathy was just plain nice. She was too nice. She was so nice that she sacrificed profit to shower her team with love and gifts. She forfeited her own paycheck and used her own money for the good of her staff. In as kind and gentle a way as I could muster, after my series of noes and nopes, I explained to Cathy why profitability had to come first. The longevity of her business was at risk; everything she had worked for, and everything she had sacrificed, could be for nothing.

Cathy needed to prioritize her time and become more aware of her revenue so that she could find the confident entrepreneur, businesswoman, and boss who had been inside her all along. She *was* strong; she just didn't know it yet. She put everyone and everything before herself, and only cut herself a check if there was anything left. She tried so hard to make others happy, even if it meant forgoing her own happiness for the sake of theirs.

At that time, she had no idea that, in less than a year, she would nearly triple the number of employees in her company. She had never imagined that she would begin to value herself enough to take care of number one first. She had never dreamed of a day when she knew for sure that her employees felt lucky to work at a practice like hers, when she didn't have to sacrifice personally in order to try and keep them happy. And at that time, Cathy had never considered that there would come a day when she started referring to her own team as employees, putting the business's diagnosis first, and, for the first time ever, turning a profit.

It wasn't a quick process. It took months before Cathy started to see the positive effects of her hard work. But in less than a year, Cathy went from rarely considering the fact that she could be successful to demanding success through her hard work and perseverance. She's the epitome of digging in without being afraid of committing to a process. She recognized the challenges she faced and approached them with confidence. She worked through each and every one of her practice's diagnoses, one at a time, always focusing her energy and efforts on the one that would make the biggest impact on her goal. I don't attribute her success to my help, but I couldn't be prouder of her for digging in her heels and becoming a confident entrepreneur.

Profit can be hard. Shifting to an entrepreneurial mindset can be a challenge. It can make you question your philanthropic heart. I'm telling you this now because I want you to know it can be done. Allow yourself time to think, give yourself grace, and don't give up. Cathy didn't, and she's in a much better place than before, when she wasn't thinking of profit first.

WHAT YOU TAKE, NOT WHAT YOU MAKE

Profit might arguably be the element of business that is most important, least understood, and most neglected by entrepreneurs. There is often confusion about the money that comes in (gross sales) versus the money you have left over after expenses (net profit). Profit is the money you *take from* your business, not what you *make in* your business.

I was talking to a practice owner about profit and he said to me, "I don't want my business to turn a profit." I paused, started to speak, paused again to compose myself, and asked why with curiosity.

"There are two main reasons. One, if I turn a profit, I will have to pay taxes. And two, my business can't afford to take a profit." Again I started to speak, paused, filtered my response, and carried on in an attempt to understand. Unfortunately, these are just two of the many erroneous profit-related ideas that I hear from entrepreneurs, and they hurt my heart every single time.

Every February, at my annual tax meeting with my CPA, I find myself asking the same question over and over.

"Jon, why are all these business owners boasting about not having to pay taxes while I need to sell my firstborn?" (By the way, he knows I'm joking for two reasons. I would never actually sell my child, and since I use the Profit First method developed by Mike Michalowicz, author of *Profit First*, I already have the money to pay my tax obligation in full every year.)

Again and again, he chuckles and says, "If you're paying taxes, you're making money. If you're making money, you should be paying taxes."

My client who didn't want to take a profit was afraid to allocate any of his gross revenue to that category because he thought he might need the money to operate. If he took it for himself, it wouldn't be there if he needed it. Because of his fear of "not having enough," he neglected an incredibly important aspect of entrepreneurship. You owe yourself and your business profitability. You deserve it. Operating a business without *taking* any of *your* money is ludicrous, and you deserve better.

You assume all the risk, pull all the late nights, and sacrifice time with your family that you will never get back. If there's no money to take, why are you doing it? As you've heard me say already, the goal of your practice must be profitability. If you get nothing from this chapter but that concept, I will be satisfied. Your efforts, your interventions, and your time should all have one goal, and that is profitability.

A couple of years ago, I was relaxing on a family member's sofa as we all prepared to dive into the carved turkey and devour my personal favorite, the stuffing. It was Christmas, and I was patiently waiting for a big plate of those fixings, along with some country ham and homemade mac and cheese. My kids were running around like wild animals. I kept an eye out for my little one, who likes to adorn walls with art. It wouldn't be the first time she'd been caught red-handed decorating a bedroom wall with a Sharpie. If you ever buy a home in Somerset, Kentucky that has the word "Lennon" written on a wall with a backwards "e," it used to be my house. She has marked her territory in every home we've ever lived in. As all of this played out in front of me, I kept my eyes on the kids, but my ears were tuned into something else.

A conversation was stirring between some relatives, including one who is part owner of a large family-run business in our region. He boasted about how he didn't have to pay taxes. For a split second I was impressed—and then I heard it. Jon's voice inside my head. "If you're making money, you're paying taxes."

Yes! If you're not paying taxes, you're not actually profiting, and if your business is not profitable, what's the point? I sat quietly and made a mental note to call Jon after the holidays for further reassurance, but I knew what he was going to say—the same thing he says every year.

All too often, I see people spend money on things to avoid paying taxes; which is fine, if you actually need those things. But spending money just to spend money is an expense and you're racking them up, my friend. You know your business is profitable if one of two things happen: One, the cash stays in the bank, or two, it is distributed to the business's shareholders (a.k.a. *you*).

Profit keeps your business in business. If it weren't for profit, you would struggle constantly to keep the lights on and the employees paid. You would have the persistent, nagging feeling that you were about to lose it all. You would constantly live on the other side of confidence because, if just a couple things were to go awry, what would save your behind?

Without profitability, we act out of fear. When we make decisions from a place of uncertainty, we take feeling-based actions that, as you know, will always fail us. We must make decisions from a place of confidence. With this system, you will find that confidence—and I will be here to support you along the way.

THE FIVE CORE NEEDS IN THE PROFIT LEVEL

In this chapter, I'll share the five Core Needs your company must satisfy in order to have a rock-solid **PROFIT** level on the HHN. In my work with Cathy, we moved through these needs one by one, calling each one a diagnosis and treating it appropriately. It wasn't always pretty, but we had a clear direction and were able to shore up nearly every diagnosis in her **PROFIT** level. It didn't happen in a linear fashion, either. We started with what we identified first, not with number one and working our way through to number five. Each time we satisfied a need, we went back and completed the diagnostic assessment again, starting with **SALES**. We let the results tell us where we should focus next.

PROFIT LEVEL

1 **Debt Eradication**
Do you consistently remove debt from your practice rather than accumulate it?

2 **Margin Health**
Does each of your offerings have a healthy profit margin, and do you continually seek ways to improve these margins?

3 **Appointment Frequency**
Do your clients repeatedly and regularly schedule with you as recommended in their treatment plans?

4 **Profitable Leverage**
When debt is used, is it used to generate predictable, increased volume and profitability?

5 **Cash Reserves**
Does your practice have enough cash reserves to cover all expenses for three months or longer?

DIAGNOSIS #1:
Debt Eradication

Question: *Do you consistently remove debt from your practice rather than accumulate it?*

It wasn't until a couple of years ago that I actually had the confidence to take on debt. I grew up in a middle-class family, doing middle-class things with middle-class debt. I didn't witness my parents or grandparents spending more than they had in their checking accounts to satisfy their wants, or use debt to leverage a business. My parents weren't entrepreneurs; they were employees. They worked hard and provided for me. The old saying "You have to spend money to make money"? I never saw that come to fruition. If we needed something, we worked until we had the money to buy it. "If we can't afford it, we don't need it," Poppy would always say.

As I grew up, I followed suit. If I needed something, I worked until I could afford it. When I wanted to start my own business, I borrowed $600 for a couch to furnish my office. I pulled all of the other furniture and decorations from spare bedrooms, the garage, or the Goodwill. Going into debt to start a business didn't even seem like an option. Fast forward nearly ten years and I'm just now understanding how to use debt to leverage profitability. As a result of that understanding, I've purchased several commercial properties and used them in a way that was profitable from day one. I know I've piqued your curiosity, but don't worry; I'll tell you all my secrets later in this chapter. For now, it's important that you know it took a first experience for me to gain the confidence to do it again and again.

Hopefully this never happens, but if there ever comes a point when I can't pay my mortgages, then I can't *afford* my mortgages. This would mean that I have more expenses than I have money, and zero profit. If you're unable to pay your bills without incurring debt (credit cards, loans, etc.) your

PROFIT level needs are not being met. Therefore, you have a positive diagnosis somewhere in that level.

People overthink this, but it's actually very simple. When your **PROFIT** level needs are unmet you have three choices: increase prices, cut costs, or do both. These are the only three options you have. If you can't pay your bills, you must not take on new debt. That being said, you may not like the interventions for this diagnosis—but they are necessary. They're more than necessary; they're critical. You must have profitability to have a sustainable practice.

> **Presenting Symptoms:** Your business may have a Debt Eradication diagnosis if there's no money left to go to **PROFIT** after you cover all your expenses, or if, in a case where you take your profit first, there isn't enough money left to pay your expenses after you pay yourself. It sounds straightforward, and it is. This diagnosis may leave you feeling anxious in the pit of your stomach, and like you might need to seek out more debt to cover monthly operating expenses. You may even worry that if you don't land a big contract or double your billable hours, your practice might be doomed.

> **Possible Interventions:** To eradicate debt in your practice, start by compiling a list of your expenses. Assess the necessity of each and—even if only temporarily—start removing the debt that is not leveraging your profit margin. If you employ an office manager, have them look at the same list with no input from you and determine what is necessary and what is not. I say this because sometimes you will be emotionally tied to certain expenses, and you need someone who is rational and objective to hold you accountable. Have your office manager, your assistant, or anyone in your practice call regarding each

of your recurring expenses to negotiate your rates. My office manager, did this and continues to do it each year. She saved us over $3,000 when she first negotiated all of our monthly expenses. It's amazing what can happen when you ask.

TREATMENT PLAN:
Debt Eradication

1. **Presenting Problem:** Sara finds herself relying on her credit cards to pull her out of any financial surprises that come her way. Before she knows it, she has racked up quite a large amount of debt, with an interest rate that is higher than she is comfortable carrying.

2. **Diagnosis:** Debt Eradication

3. **Strengths:** Sara keeps track of her financials on a monthly basis. She relies on her bookkeeper to reconcile the accounts, but she does a good job of drawing conclusions based on what she sees.

4. **Baseline:** Sara has a current balance of $24,000 on one credit card that she rolled the other three into.

5. **Goal:** Sara will pay off the credit card total of $24,000 within six months.

6. **Interventions:**

   1. Sara will complete a new assessment of her financials and allocate a higher percentage of revenue toward paying off debt.

   2. In order to make room for the additional revenue to go to her operating expenses, she will cancel all her unnecessary subscription-based services.

7. **Plan for Progress:** Based on the current incoming revenue and the percentage Sara will be contributing toward paying down the

balance on her credit card, she will be able to pay it off within six months. The savings on unnecessary subscriptions will be a bonus and make an even bigger impact on the debt. Sara will continue to evaluate her progress monthly, always seeking ways to contribute a higher portion of revenue toward paying off the credit card balance. Sara knows that the quicker she pays off her debt, the more money she will save in interest.

DIAGNOSIS #2:
Margin Health

Question: *Does each of your offerings have a healthy profit margin, and do you continually seek ways to improve these margins?*

When I first started consulting, I charged my clients the same amount as my hourly rate for clinical work. When I think about it now, I wonder what on earth I was doing. It probably went back to a lack of confidence. Without a strong understanding of the value of my time and talent, I set myself up for a lot of work and not much profit. You may think you're 100% profitable if you're providing a service like consulting, coaching, or counseling, but you're not. Your time, education, experience, and skills are valuable. It's hard to put a price on such intangibles, but if you value your 55-minute counseling session at $100, you might as well expect that somewhere between 15 and 30% of that will go toward overhead. This does not even include the time you put into the service. We must consider all of these things when we assign a dollar amount to our offerings.

I started out charging much less for consulting services than I do now. I also have hundreds more clients now than I did when I started, and a long waiting list. Many times, people perceive your value based on what you charge. I thought I was being respectful of my clients by charging less, but I was just diluting the perception of the value I provided. Now, I run a very affordable membership program[7] for group practice owners. However, when offered my small-group or one-on-one coaching experiences,[8] which are between $5,000 and $25,000, they will choose the more expensive option almost every single time.

People want you to charge them your value. They want you to be profitable. They want you to make money. After all, they come to you for a reason. They need help, and they know that the only way you can keep helping them is if you are profitable. If you're not confident enough in your offerings to charge a premium for them, I encourage you to go back to the basics. Look at that offering and ask yourself how you can make it stronger, better, and different. What would it take to get to a place where you could confidently increase your price by 20, 30, or even 100%? That's where I want you to be.

Wendy Maynard, marketing strategist and business coach, says *value* is the key to pricing your services. And value, as it turns out, is an incredibly relative concept. She says, "People tend to perceive companies with higher pricing as more prestigious and, as a result, more desirable. They also assume that a high price indicates that the product or service quality is high as well."[9] Higher prices can cause consumers to place a higher value on your services.

Now, some of you may be feeling a tickle of guilt in the back of your mind as you entertain this idea, but I promise you, it is not sleazy or underhanded. People want to pay you to solve their problems, and you need a healthy profit margin in order to keep helping.

---

[7] Mindsight Partners: https://www.mindsightpartners.com

[8] VIP Coaching—Entrepreneurial Accelerator: https://www.kaseycompton.com/vipofferings

[9] Maynard, Wendy. "Why You Should Charge Higher Prices for Your Services: Premium Pricing." December 16, 2019, https://www.wendymaynard.com/the-surprising-reason-you-should-charge-a-premium-price-for-your-services/

Presenting Symptoms: In the healthcare industry, one of our biggest expenses is compensation for our providers. If you're in the mental health space, it's fairly standard to pay employees between 40 and 55% of the insurance reimbursement or fee collected for the service they provide, while the industry standard for independent contractors is about 60%. Unlike other industries with healthy margins, mental health starts out pretty low. If you have a diagnosis of Margin Health, you're likely to feel that there isn't enough left after expenses are paid.

You may have some pay periods when there isn't enough in the bank to cover your payroll. You may not have enough left over to give out those Christmas bonuses you've been wanting to give. There may not be enough to invest in retirement plans, and you may wonder if you can continue to contribute 50% to your employees' healthcare premiums. You could find yourself struggling to come up with ways to retain your staff. They may be leaving to seek out higher-paying positions somewhere else, but you know you are giving as much as you can.

Possible Interventions: As I sit here and type this section on Margin Health, my own wheels are turning. This is a category I always come back to in my practice. Our margins stink, and that's *not* because of anything we're doing wrong. It's the reality of the situation I am in as a competitive insurance-based practice. If you're bound by insurance rates, you will have to force yourself to think creatively. If you're not, if yours is a fee-for-service practice, the simplest first step is to raise your rates. You will see an instant increase in your profit margin with that one action. Don't be tempted to talk yourself out of it, thinking that your clients will go somewhere else if you raise your rates. They won't—at least, not enough to impact you. You will make up the difference with the higher margins from the ones who stay.

For insurance-based practices, let's start with simple and logical steps. Request a rate increase, do it every six months, and be persistent. I know companies who have had success with rate increase after rate increase simply because they asked and showed justification based on the experience and specialties of their staff.

Streamline and automate systems and processes to cut costs and increase margins. My team and I created Systemizer School,[10] which walks business owners through the entire process of increasing profitability through efficiency and order. We've successfully helped practice owners save at least 10% of their overhead within four weeks. My office staff and I constantly brainstorm ways to improve our margin health so we can pay our clinical staff the highest amount possible. After all, they deserve that for all of the hard work they do and their dedication to their clients.

Since our practice is bound by insurance, and in many ways our hands are tied, I will create a passive income stream that can be 100% passed along to my clinicians. With minimal startup costs, the buy-in and participation of my team should give them each a salary increase of about $4,000 per year. Is this idea unconventional? Yes! But if it can add an additional $4,000 to the annual salary of each of my staff for only a few hours of up-front costs, I think it's worth it.

---

[10] Systemizer School: https://www.mindsightpartners.com/systemizer-school

TREATMENT PLAN:
Margin Health

1. **Presenting Problem:** My group practice, Mindsight Behavioral Group, has profit margins that are fixed due to our being an insurance-based practice. We want to pay the providers more, but since we're insurance-based, the only way to make more money is to cut costs. We need all of our current support staff, so eliminating positions is not an option. We've already streamlined and systemized every process so that no funds or effort are wasted.

2. **Diagnosis:** Margin Health

3. **Strengths:** Mindsight has a resourceful team of administrative and support staff. We are creative in our approach and open to new ideas.

4. **Baseline:** Mindsight would like to pay its clinical providers 12% more per billable service. However, there is no more room in the current margin to make that happen.

5. **Goal:** Mindsight will create a passive or additional revenue stream that will generate enough revenue to equal the 12% increase needed to justify our providers' rate increase.

6. **Interventions:**

   1. Mindsight will capitalize on its strength of its membership community, Mindsight Partners. Mindsight Partners does not yet have a clinical component, so this will be a perfect time to add one.

   2. Mindsight's clinicians will provide a monthly "insider scoop" Q&A, in which they answer questions from practice owners about the thought processes and preferences of clinicians, and use the profit generated to increase their own salaries. Essentially, they will

take what they are already doing in their work with Mindsight and teach other group practices to implement the same clinical strategies.

3. The clinicians interested in participating will split 100% of the revenue generated equally.

7. **Plan for Progress:** Since the coordination of this program will be the most time-consuming piece, that will start immediately. The providers who choose to participate will meet weekly until the program is developed, then review the effectiveness and the partners' response to it on a monthly basis. Adjustments will be made as needed.

DIAGNOSIS #3:
Appointment Frequency

Question: *Do your clients repeatedly and regularly schedule with you based on the recommendations of their clinical treatment plan?*

The goal of appointment frequency is to get the same clients to schedule with you on a regular basis in order to meet the clinical goals in their treatment plan. A step beyond that is to utilize existing clients in multiple offerings without ever compromising the quality of the work you provide. You've probably heard the term "client acquisition cost" (CAC). This is the cost you accrue in order to get a new client. About a year ago, I consulted with a digital marketing firm that tried to sell me on an SEO package. As I sat in the corner of a local restaurant, chowing down on my avocado hoagie and watching their presentation, I had one burning question.

What is the client acquisition cost for my *practice?*

Little did I know, digital marketing experts don't like to answer that question. The marketing firm representative didn't want to tell me, but after she fumbled around the question for a moment or two, I got my number. In my small town, within my industry, a typical CAC is $100. This means I pay close to that or more for every new client who comes into our practice. For right now, think about it like this: If $100 is my company's marketing cost to get one new client in the door, why do I focus on more new clients when I can utilize the clients I currently have and maximize their financial value to my practice? Why don't I create systems to ensure that these clients are seen regularly and are in compliance with the frequency and intensity of their treatment recommendations? Why don't I assess these clients' needs for other internal services before we spend money trying to get more clients?

Most of us tell ourselves that we need more clients when really, we just need to utilize and serve the ones we have. We are more profitable when the same clients return to their providers week after week to work toward their wellness goals. When they are successful and feel better, we all win.

In fact, we want even more than that. We want them to keep coming back throughout the course of their lifetimes. We want them to love us so much that they refer everyone they know. We want them to bring their kids and their partners. This is how we lower our customer acquisition cost, increase our transaction frequency, improve our profit margins, and reach our practice's goal of profitability.

Presenting Symptoms: Your practice may have an Appointment Frequency diagnosis if clients come once and don't come back. This means your retention rates are low. You may have this problem if you have lots of new leads coming in but notice that the schedule is bare when you look a week or two out. Are your providers recommending follow-up visits and managing clients' expectations? Do new clients have a clear understanding that their best chance to reach their treatment goals is to comply with provider recommendations and participate in interventions to the best of their ability?

Possible Interventions: With an Appointment Frequency diagnosis, you need to remember the word *accountability*. You must create a system for holding your support staff and clinical providers accountable for scheduling follow-up appointments. Does your staff understand how many sessions it takes for your practice to break even after acquiring one client? Have you shown them the customer acquisition cost formula?[11] When I told my therapists that it took 11 sessions to break even after acquiring a single client, they thought I was crazy! I explained that our marketing cost to acquire one client is approximately $100. On top of that cost, we must add operating expenses, which are typically 25% of gross. Then, of course, the therapist wants to be paid, so we add that in as well. Then there is the revenue to set aside for taxes and, before you know it, it takes 11 sessions for the company to break even and become profitable. When your providers understand how much work goes into getting one client, and that the responsibility to keep that client falls to them, they will start to develop a greater appreciation for the process.

It's very easy for healthcare entrepreneurs to answer yes to this question. "Of course our patients come back to us repeatedly," they say. But is that true? Many are shocked to find out it's not always the case.

Without a sense of accountability for this diagnosis, it will be nearly impossible to create effective interventions. That said, an additional possible

---

[11] You can find a handy reference in FTN: QuickStart at https://www.kaseycompton.com/ftn

intervention for an Appointment Frequency diagnosis is to use a dashboard to track client retention rates and/or patient utilization.

TREATMENT PLAN:
Appointment Frequency

1. **Presenting Problem:** Carrie seems to have a problem with her therapists keeping their schedules full. She knows there are quite a few new clients coming into the practice, but it seems like they disappear after their first appointment. She knows that in order to maintain her desired profit margin, this has to be addressed.

2. **Diagnosis:** Appointment Frequency

3. **Strengths:** The practice has built a great reputation, especially in an area where insurance-based practices are the norm. Carrie's practice is all fee-for-service and she wants to keep it that way. Her providers do great clinical work, and she understands numbers and dashboards well.

4. **Baseline:** Some investigation reveals that after the initial appointment, only 40% of clients are coming back weekly. The remaining 60%, which makes up the bulk of the caseload, is only randomly scheduling appointments. Carrie also notices that one clinician's rates are much better than those of anyone else in the practice.

5. **Goal:** 75% of new clients scheduled within the next 60 days will return for weekly sessions for at least eight weeks.

6. **Interventions:**
   1. Carrie will schedule a meeting with her high-performing clinician as soon as possible. She will find out what her process is for scheduling recurring follow-up sessions with clients and convert the process into a standard operating procedure for the practice.

2. She will begin tracking all of the metrics, including date of initial appointment, assigned clinician, and appointment frequency recommendation versus appointment frequency outcome.

7. **Plan for Progress:** Carrie will meet with her clinicians weekly to discuss each client's case and the recommended frequency of sessions (weekly, biweekly, or monthly). She will monitor this closely every week for the next two months and make modifications if necessary.

DIAGNOSIS #4:
Profitable Leverage

Question: *When debt is used, is it used to generate predictable, increased profitability?*

The type of practice you have will determine the amount of debt you accumulated at the start of your business. Many practices cost nearly nothing to start, like the $600 I spent on a couch for my mental health practice. Other practices, like chiropractic offices, may have to buy larger equipment such as X-ray machines, hydromassage units, or exam tables before the practice opens. In most cases, these are necessary expenses that will most definitely generate profit in a very short period of time.

Good debt leverage is when one dollar borrowed results in a quick and predictable dollar-plus returned. In the healthcare space, debt is often used in different ways. Since we're not in an industry that invests $10,000 to $20,000 in monthly ad spending for a Facebook campaign, our profitable leverage might look a little different. You may see our industry spend money on Google AdWords campaigns or geofencing in order to easily attract clients who use online search engines.

In 2017, I was encouraged to move to a much larger building—which I did, hesitantly. It was nearly eight times the space and approximately five times the cost of my previous space. I knew I wanted to grow the practice, but I wasn't sure I wanted to go into debt to do it. Nevertheless, I signed a 5-year lease and immediately doubled our gross revenue because it had twenty-three therapy rooms (as opposed to four at the smaller space).

After about a year at the newer, larger location, I made the decision to go into debt by more than $1,000,000 to buy the property rather than lease it. Although we're still in debt to the bank for the purchase, I'm generating a 50% profit margin when you take into consideration the rent my group practice pays to my property company, revenue from the consulting business, and revenue from the hair salon. Although I have not yet recouped the total cost of my investment, I'm still yielding a 50% margin, which I'll take any day of the week.

> **Presenting Symptoms:** If you find yourself with a Profitable Leverage diagnosis, you may have incurred debt to solve problems. Or, you may be considering taking on debt in order to make a much-needed investment in your business. Perhaps you're out of physical space and need to rent a larger one. Maybe you're not generating enough new patients through your website and need a new one. Or maybe you want to launch a new service but need to take out a small line of credit to pay for the policy and procedures manual. You might even need some cash to help front the costs for a book you've been dreaming about writing.

> **Possible Interventions:** You complete a risk assessment or even a cost analysis breakdown. You must make sure that the debt you're about to incur will turn to profit as quickly as possible. The longer you hang onto debt, the less profitable it is

because you have less leverage. You test your theory by starting small. Instead of purchasing an entire space, try adding one office and see what kind of margin you can create. If you can make money off of one room, imagine how much you can make on 23.

TREATMENT PLAN:
Profitable Leverage

1. **Presenting Problem:** Mindsight Behavioral Group hit its capacity when its 4-room office suite filled up completely. Providers use the offices during all hours of the day, and there are virtually no more opportunities for growth.

2. **Diagnosis:** Profitable Leverage

3. **Strengths:** Mindsight has always been pretty nimble. Its employees are resourceful and aren't afraid to think outside of the box. When they lock onto a goal, they always rise to the challenge. Up until this point, their overhead has been extremely low, so their profit margins were good. They have managed to accumulate a nice little nest egg of profit.

4. **Baseline:** With 4 therapy rooms available for 8 hours per day, there are a total of 32 hours per day available for client sessions, or 160 hours per week. If the average session is $100, Mindsight's capacity for gross revenue is $16,000 per week.

5. **Goal:** Mindsight will increase its capacity to 920 sessions per week, with a goal of being at 70% capacity.

6. **Interventions:**
   1. Since 70% capacity is 644 sessions, and one provider can see 25 in a week, it will take 26 therapists to meet that goal.

2. The hiring committee will post an ad for new providers, with a goal of hiring a total of 26.

3. Productivity reports will be generated weekly to track where the business is in terms of reaching the 70% capacity goal.

7. **Plan for Progress:** Metrics will be tracked, and this goal will be evaluated on a monthly basis.

DIAGNOSIS #5:
Cash Reserves

Question: *Does your practice have enough cash reserves to cover all expenses for three months or longer?*

I know what you're thinking. Do cash reserves include payroll? What if I have an employee model versus an independent contractor model? If you have a model in which you pay your clinical providers before the reimbursement from an insurance payer, then these cash reserves include that projected salary. If you pay your providers once the company has been reimbursed, you will only need to calculate expenses minus labor.

Hopefully, none of us will ever need three months' worth of expenses due to an emergency or a natural disaster, but in these times, you can never be too sure. Although stashing cash doesn't sound as fun as creating a new community marketing campaign, it's just as necessary.

In my last Fix This Next small group coaching event, a practice owner from Paducah, Kentucky identified Cash Reserves as her primary business diagnosis. Over the last few years, she has worked hard to build a brand for her business and attract the right providers to support her purpose, but the missing piece remained that reserve of three months' worth of expenses. She had always known it was a missing piece and required focus, but something else always appeared more pressing on her to-do list. It wasn't until she took the HHN assessment, and saw it right there in black and white, that she knew Cash Reserves was the unmet need in her practice.

When Katie's assessment determined that Cash Reserves was the diagnosis, that was all it took for her to set a goal and bang out three months of expenses. Once she had the diagnosis and baseline data (her typical monthly expense, P&L, etc.), she was able to create a goal and interventions that would help her treat this need quickly. The treatment plan formula gave Katie a place to start and a foundation from which to hold herself accountable. More specifically, Katie wanted to save $60,000 in a vault account (a savings account that she doesn't touch) within seven months. Every two weeks she took her profit first, dumped it into her vault, and let it accrue.

In four short months, she has already nearly met her goal, hitting 83% of it as I write this sentence—and with three months left to save the last 17%. Although Katie joked that her Cash Reserves diagnosis was boring compared to some of the others, at the end of the day, her **PROFIT** level will be satisfied and she will have the financial leverage to take her practice in any direction she wants it to go.

As a result of using the HHN and the Fix This Next for Healthcare system, Katie now has money in the bank, peace of mind, and an overwhelming sense of freedom. When my team and I checked back in with her on her progress, she said she was pleased that the process of meeting her goal was so quick!

"It was question, answer, boom. No meetings, no meditating over a complex ideology," Katie said as we sat in amazement.

As much confidence as Katie felt with her first fix, she now says she's ready to go back and diagnose again. In conversation, she'll be the first to tell you that she can easily get caught up in "all the things." Some call it going down the rabbit hole or getting sidetracked, but we Kentucky girls like to call it "chasing squirrels." I can identify with Katie because I too am from Kentucky, and I too am tempted by squirrel-chasing. When given a simple tool like the HHN, Katie was able to diagnose her practice, design a treatment plan, and follow the interventions while on autopilot—no squirrel-chasing required.

> **Presenting Symptoms:** This is going to be super simple. Does your practice have between two and six times your average monthly revenue reserved? If not, this is your diagnosis.

> **Possible Interventions:** Assess your monthly expenses as they are right now. Whatever percentage you take as profit, cut it by half. Move half of your profit to a Cash Reserves account and leave the rest in your profit account. Depending on how motivated you are to meet this goal, you could move all of your profit, half of your profit, or a smaller amount. This is a plan where you can set it and forget it. You can move on to your next diagnosis as soon as you have a plan in place to continue shifting a percentage of your profits into Cash Reserves. Before you know it, you will have the reserves that will both rescue your business if it ever needs rescuing and give you the confidence to run your business from a place of empowerment.

TREATMENT PLAN:
Cash Reserves

1. **Presenting Problem:** Katie felt guilty for always neglecting her Cash Reserves. She knew it was important, but every time she sat down to structure a plan, something else seemed more urgent.
2. **Diagnosis:** Cash Reserves

3. **Strengths:** Once Katie has a plan, she's compliant and always follows through. Katie understands the importance of these Cash Reserves and is highly motivated to reach this goal.

4. **Baseline:** Katie has money saved in her practice, but none specifically dedicated to Cash Reserves.

5. **Goal:** Katie will save $60,000 in seven months.

6. **Interventions:**
   1. Katie will take the minimum profit allotment each month to build up personal cash reserves. She will take the amount of desired savings and the goal date and divide desired savings equally among the months to create a target amount to reach each month.
   2. Katie will take every opportunity to cut back on spending (travel, tech upgrades, gifts, meals, etc.) and commit to a super lean sprint to meet the goal as soon as possible.

7. **Plan for Progress:** Once Katie has set this goal, she can move on to the next since her Cash Reserves plan can run in the background while she addresses something else. Each month, after the bookkeeper reconciles her accounts, she will track her progress. She will look for ways to increase her Cash Reserve allocation to meet her goal even faster.

PROFIT IS PRIORITY

People don't mind talking about how much money their business makes in a year. They'll lead with it in mastermind groups, reference it during keynotes, and plaster it on the front page of an acquisition proposal, but they start to get a little squirmy when you mention how much *profit* the business had. Making money is not too terribly hard. You have a product or a service that people want, you tell them about it, and there's an exchange of goods or services for money. Generating a profit takes much more skill. You must be good at making money *and* keeping it, and not many people are. You must be as disciplined in maintaining your profit as you are in creating your profit.

I want you to be able to lead with your successes in the **PROFIT** level and feel confident in who you are as an entrepreneur. I want you to feel the security and confidence to continue growing your practice because your business's Core Needs are met. I want you to be able to go out there and take chances while lenders look at you with admiration. I want you to be the practice owner whose banker loves to see you coming and is practically begging you for a deal. All businesses deserve profitability, and in order to make it happen, we must first make it a priority.

Chapter Five

Create ORDER from Within

I ATTRIBUTE ALL THE SUCCESSES AND FAILURES IN MY BUSINESSES to systems. I've achieved success when I had good systems, and I've failed when I didn't. They have given me the ability to increase capacity and improve efficiency through every phase of growth. They've always been a strength for me, and I find joy in **ORDER**. Like anything, with enough practice, you can become skilled at efficiency. You don't have to have a special talent for order to be successful. You just have to have the willingness to observe and learn.

Systems are everywhere and in everything. From nature to business to the human body, they are ingrained within us. The systems that exist within our family unit are not much different from those in our work family. Have you ever thought about how you naturally implement processes to maintain order, and how each person's personality influences the way those processes are executed?

My eldest daughter, Maime, is the analytical one of the three children: the logical one, the pointer-outer of the obvious. She thrives in order and doesn't care much for chaos, just like her momma. Since she was a little girl, she has demanded structure in her routine to maintain a sense of peace. Anything that varies from the norm gives her pause. During her toddler years, interruptions in routine often threw her into a fit of tantrums, which made my life very difficult. I spent many hours carrying her surfboard-style out of public events after she lost her dang mind. She was little, she was my first, and, like her, I was learning too.

Even as an adult I feel the need for order, and, for the most part, I grew out of my tantrums. Luckily, so did Maime, but sometimes our businesses don't. Think about what *your business's* tantrums look like—those moments when tasks get lost, follow-through is nonexistent, and you seriously consider walking out the back door and never coming back. Moments when it feels easier to accept the subpar rather than fight for excellence, and moments when you find peace in the distractions. The constant wave of fires that need to be extinguished, the sense of urgency that never disappears; all this could mirror a business's tantrum. It's a humanlike way of saying, "Pay attention to me!" Just like a toddler does.

My youngest daughter, Lennon, the one who marked her territory on all my walls with a Sharpie, has quite a different take on life. While Maime is the rule-follower, Lennon takes every single opportunity to push the boundaries of others. She thrives during a challenge, whereas Maime tends to assess risk and will fold when the cards she's dealt are not that strong. Maime sets out to create order, and Lennon attempts to disrupt it, any chance she gets.

Several years back, my group practice was new. We lived in a rental, about three miles from where we live now. Lennon was just three years old at the time and beginning to find her wild and adventurous soul.

As I sat balled up on the couch, computer in my lap, I heard, "Momma, can I have some ice cweam?"

Totally underestimating her determination, I replied, "Hang on, it's in the freezer," and went back to finishing my work.

The room got quiet—awfully quiet, too quiet. That gut feeling we have when it comes to our children, well, it told me to put down the computer and go check on her.

"Lennon," I said, hoping to hear an answer so I didn't have to get up. No luck. I put the computer aside and rolled off the couch. I turned the corner and there she was: all twenty-five pounds of blonde hair, big blue eyes, and tan skin staring back at me from *on top* of my refrigerator. How she got up there, I will never be certain. But from the looks of it, she dragged the chair over from the table and used the countertop as her first step. From there, she must have opened the freezer door, wedged her little foot inside the lowest shelf, and climbed to the top. She sat there looking proud and certainly feeling accomplished. She had no other goal but to make it to the top. And that she did.

She's the free spirit in the family and doesn't take no for an answer. In her eyes, there's always a way. If you lose something, just ask Lennon. She always knows where it is. She has no sense of fear or lack of self-confidence. She enjoys every moment and loves and lives hard. While Maime will carefully think through every scenario, giving much attention to the details, Lennon operates out of simplicity. Tell her to do something and she'll do one of two things: pretend she never heard you, or find the shortest and easiest way to get the job done. At four years old, she had already outsmarted my iCloud passwords, managed to escape from a house with alarms on every single door and window, and found a way to steal cookies that were behind a locked pantry door. When you're working to achieve **ORDER** in your business, you want to channel your inner Maime and leave Lennon for the strategic interventions in Chapter Seven!

Even in my personal life, I filter most decisions through the **ORDER** lens. I used to question whether family trips would be too chaotic to even be worth it. And even now, when I'm tempted to buy something new, go on a dream vacation, or drive forty-five minutes to have dinner, I consider the fact that my children, wild and relentless, will put a strain on the process. They're like a built-in pressure test for my family's systems. Many times, this means we stay home. My **ORDER** filter provides me with the forethought to understand that, for example, in order to make it out of the house and get each child to school on time, we have to adapt the morning processes to ensure **ORDER**.

When you think about it, the daily interactions you have with your staff are much like the ones you have with your family. You have the defiant child, and the resistant employee. You have the free-spirited six-year-old, and the employee who lacks a sense of urgency. You have the rule-follower at home, and the rule-follower at the office. Think about how you manage your household. You most likely look at the strengths and weaknesses of each member and create a structure in which they will thrive. You don't set them up for failure, you position them to succeed. You will do the same thing to satisfy the foundational level of **ORDER** in your practice.

ORDER determines your capacity for growth, your scalability. When you achieve **ORDER**, your business will run without you, and it will run with efficiency. Gone are the days when you must call all the shots, be present at every morning meeting, or point out all the problems for everyone in the building to see. **ORDER** will grant you the efficiency needed to further reduce operating expenses and increase profit margins. It will give you the freedom to scale your practice in a way that doesn't feel like more work. It will give you back the time you want to spend with the ones you love.

It is a way of thinking that not everyone can do with ease. Some fall right into **ORDER**'s lap; it comes naturally and they do it well. These folks are aware of their surroundings, ask themselves what would make the most sense in any given situation, and only challenge rules of thumb when they completely go against what their instincts say is right. Others will do only what "feels" right. They base their decisions on what elicits an emotional reaction, and often come across as free spirits.

My husband and I also operate from opposite ends of the **ORDER** spectrum. I am the analytical thinker, like Maime, while he is the free spirit, like

Lennon. It takes me no longer than fifteen minutes to get all three children and our German shepherd ready and out the door in the morning, while it takes him at least forty-five (and he still sends Lennon to kindergarten with only one white knee sock on).

Creating order is about taking what you already do and making it more efficient. It means increasing capacity through the art of streamlining and automating the existing systems in your business. "ORDER is a basic level in the HHN, requiring the improvement and dissemination of systems to achieve predictable outcomes." This quote came from the original *Fix This Next*, and man, it's good! This is why we work so hard to achieve order.

Do you remember the goal of your practice? Profitability. The best predictor of future behavior is past behavior, and this is why order works. In business, the only way we can make meaning out of the data we collect is by seeking out patterns. The more consistent we can make our input, the more we are able to predict the output, should we continue to implement the same actions and interventions.

We must capture the systems we already use based on logic and common sense, but when they don't yet exist, we must create them. The biggest problem I see is that healthcare entrepreneurs lose sight of their goal. They forget that all actions should move them toward profitability. When we lose sight of our goal, the systems and processes that help us to achieve order go right down the toilet. This is evidenced when you watch yourself or your team go through the motions to complete a boatload of tasks even though only a fraction of them are relevant to improving profitability.

When I put my entire office staff through the Systemizer School[12] program, their daily tasks and their assumptions about the position they held

---

[12] Systemizer School is an eight-week program held twice a year for business owners who meet the application requirements. We basically systemize the shit out of your business. https://www.mindsightpartners.com/systemizer-school

in the company were challenged. Although I'm sure they cursed me when I was not around, they now appreciate the push. They have become more successful in their roles because their tasks are aligned not only with their talents, but also with the specific goals of their positions and the goal of the company. It's a win-win. They're happier, more productive, and more efficient, and I can step away from the business when I want a break.

While I enjoy beautiful sunrises and evening walks on a beach on the East Coast, the systems in my practice bear the brunt of the workload. As I enjoy watching my geriatric dog frolic in the ocean, my business keeps on running. As I enjoy delicious fried green tomatoes with Southern pimento cheese from Low Country Produce, my business keeps on going. As I browse every single nook and cranny of Nevermore Books in Beaufort, South Carolina, my business continues to make money. Because we achieved **ORDER**, my support staff are confident in their roles and empowered to take on any and all responsibilities in my absence. That's what I want for you.

ESTABLISHING ORDER ON THE INSIDE

Order starts from within: within the company, the department, the system, the process, and the person. It is possible to achieve the kind of order that allows you the freedom to live life on your own terms. There was a time when I felt proud of myself for making a good hire. I had looked for someone with charisma and charm, someone who could gain the staff's trust and be a catalyst for positive change in the practice. It felt like the right fit at the outset, but over the course of time I realized it was not so good. Sometimes the people we put in leadership roles are there because we see them as they *could* be while ignoring the reality that they may never get there. They may never live up to the potential we see because we've set them up for roles that may not align with the visions they have for themselves.

We must start with people first. When we hire new employees, their ability to follow processes, work deliberately toward a goal, and understand efficiency should be at the forefront of our criteria. Employees who do not have personalities capable of this type of thinking will derail your efforts toward systemization. If you're looking at existing employees, this is the time to go back to the beginning and teach these concepts. You must design an organizational structure that includes people who embrace processes and understand their necessity for achieving efficiency. You must be able to identify the natural-born **ORDER** creators in your business and consider including this quality in their job description.

A perfect example of this is Mindsight's former client care coordinator, Bubbly Britany. Britany is an amazing employee, one who will do absolutely anything you tell her to do. She will not question authority; she will smile, maybe giggle a little, and do what you ask. Well, that's how she used to be. Recently, Britany was promoted to human resources director because she demonstrated the skills, the talent, and the motivation to grow both professionally and personally. It wasn't until then that she went from Bubbly Britany to Badass Britany (a.k.a. BA Britany) because she was willing to step up, step out, and challenge herself to be better. She's now being groomed for the highest-level position within our company, chief operating officer. She demonstrates a talent for training and recognizing inefficiencies, and has the confidence to speak up and challenge others. She's always looking for a better way.

After a frustrating first attempt to create a business that would continue to run when key employees were unavailable, I realized it wasn't going to work; I just could never figure out why. After using the Fix This Next system, we realized it was because we weren't ready. I hadn't shored up the **SALES** and **PROFIT** levels so that my **ORDER** level could flourish. My team and I continued to be distracted. Every time we started the process of systemizing the practice, a catastrophe would occur that consumed all of our attention and resources. It wasn't until I read *Fix This Next* and implemented the system that we realized: clockworking a business too soon will leave you feeling frustrated and inefficient. You must make sure your sales and profit are in order... get it? **SALES**, **PROFIT**, *then* **ORDER**!

You can have a business that runs without you. There's just one catch. You must satisfy the needs in all five categories of **ORDER**. "If you're getting shit done, it means what you are getting done is shit. Stop doing for your business, and start designing your business to run without you, permanently," says Mike in *Fix This Next*. He's right.

ORDER LEVEL

1

Systemization
Do you have an ongoing, working model to reduce bottlenecks, congestion points, and inefficiencies?

2

Role Alignment
Are people's roles and responsibilities matched with their talents?

3

Outcome Delegation
Do the people closest to the problem feel empowered to resolve it?

4

Linchpin Redundancy
Is your practice designed to operate unabated when critical employees are unavailable?

5

Problem-solving Solutions
Do you and your team have an effective working model for solving problems as they arise?

DIAGNOSIS #1:
Systemization

Question: *Do you have an ongoing, working model to reduce bottlenecks, congestion points, and inefficiencies?*

I put a lot of effort into teaching my team the language to use to communicate about order. Not too long ago, I got an email from my human resources director, BA Britany. The first sentence was, "I've become a big bottleneck and I need your help." I knew it pained her terribly to send an email like this, but a big smile came over my face. I couldn't help it. I was proudest of the fact that we were all starting to communicate using specific, meaningful language, and only slightly less proud that she recognized the fact that she was a bottleneck *and* needed help. Things had to be bad, really bad, before BA Britany sent such an email. I'd even go out on a limb and say that she probably started typing it several times before actually hitting send.

What BA Britany didn't know was that I had seen this coming. In an effort to help her coworkers, she made herself available to them eight hours a day. While *their* work was getting done, many thanks to her, *hers* wasn't because there wasn't enough time for everything. If the office manager asked for help, Britany stopped what she was doing and came to her rescue. If the billing coordinator had a problem, BA Britany saved the day. She acted as if she had all the time in the world, but in reality, she only had eight hours in a day minus lunch, not to mention the time she needed to eat, pee, and go for a little stretch every now and then.

The problem became evident when I checked in with her on the status of tasks I had personally assigned to her a couple of weeks before. They weren't done, and her excuse was time. I asked how she prioritized tasks, and found that she didn't. She addressed the one problem that was making the most noise at any given time. This kept her busy, sure, but it didn't help her reach her hiring and retention goal. In fact, it was taking her in the opposite direction of her goal. So, it had to change.

After a gentle reminder, BA Britany was able to create order within her schedule, blocking out chunks of time to complete certain tasks on certain days in order of priority. She put forth tremendous effort; however, the majority of it was wasted on tasks that were not even that important. She was still doing the wrong tasks at the wrong times and in the wrong order of priority. I offered the HHN diagnostic assessment to her, and it became her compass—and everything changed.

Presenting Symptoms: If you have a diagnosis of Systemization, you will notice multiple symptoms. For example, you may often see yourself getting sucked into several processes at the same time because you are the one everyone calls on for everything, from needing toilet paper to needing to hire and fire. Some of your processes have way too many steps, and your employees get tripped up by them and make mistakes. Things take too much time, and you may not even realize it until you start diagnosing. In a nutshell, your practice depends on you. All day, every day, you receive emails ranging from requests to approve time off to requests to discuss patient details. You move from healer to entrepreneur and back again throughout the day, wearing an assortment of hats.

Possible Interventions: The first step in cleaning up complicated and convoluted systems is to capture them. Get them down on paper and start looking at them through an objective lens. Apply for our flagship Systemizer School,[13] which will walk you through the process of creating systems step by step, day by day, until you achieve order in your practice.

---

[13] Systemizer School: https://www.mindsightpartners.com/systemizer-school

TREATMENT PLAN:
Systemization

1. **Presenting Problem:** Britany found herself being roped into all sorts of conversations by phone and via email and text. Her office staff had lots of questions, and she never seemed to be able to get any of her own work done because someone always needed help. Britany struggled to meet the deadlines set forth by the practice owner because she was pulled in too many directions by her team.

2. **Diagnosis:** Systemization

3. **Strengths:** Britany has great insight and understands what is and what isn't working well at Mindsight Behavioral Group. She has a support staff that is teachable and willing to try new things. She is empowered to solve problems and create solutions in her position as human resources director.

4. **Baseline:** Britany oversees the front office department and is working on systemizing that area. She has been helping to make changes and streamline each of the processes, but the team is still unable to work independently. She spends approximately four hours per day attending to questions and supporting this department.

5. **Goal:** Britany will spend no more than one hour per day assisting the front office department.

6. **Interventions:**
   1. Britany will develop standard operating procedures for the front office and encourage them to solve problems independently.
   2. She will create a color-coded system that tells the staff what is important for them to do on their own (green),

when to wait for assistance (yellow), and when to stop
what they're doing and ask a supervisor immediately
(red).

3. She will set designated times to work with the staff,
helping them with their yellow-coded questions. This
will batch all of the problems into a prearranged time-
frame, thereby reducing the opportunity for bottlenecks to form.

7. **Plan for Progress:** Britany will give herself one week to complete the standard operating procedures and share them with her
team. She will then reevaluate their process with this new system
weekly, troubleshooting as necessary.

DIAGNOSIS #2:
Role Alignment

Question: *Are people's roles and responsibilities matched with
their talents?*

Please don't learn this the hard way. When I first started my practice
back in 2015, I created job descriptions and then tried to fit square pegs
(employees) into the round holes (positions). As a result, I had high turnover and set myself up for failure. I remember questioning my expectations, wondering if they were just too high. *How hard can it be? I mean,
I gave them an entire twenty-three-page process for how to complete one
task.* Now I can't help but giggle when I think about it. I thought my process was the best, and because it worked for me, I assumed it would work
for my staff. What I realized was, the only thing that worked was giving
them twenty-three reasons to hate me! The moment I decided to set goals
and allowed my staff to achieve them in their own way was game-chang-
ing. This is not to say that I didn't come in and help them streamline and

automate their processes, but when I allowed them to create the steps in a way that felt good to them, they were much more effective.

Role Alignment is a constantly evolving process within a company. Just as people change, their interests change, and so do their needs. We must ensure that each employee is best suited for the task we've placed before them if we want to be certain to get the most out of the talent they bring to the table.

Presenting Symptoms: Things just feel messy, balls are dropped, and important tasks fall through the cracks. It appears that identified problems are not resolved, and the pieces are not coming together as you envisioned. You coach your employees, recommend areas for improvement, and create performance improvement plans, but nothing seems to work. You put forth the same amount of effort with no actual change, no results. Your employees are now frustrated and overwhelmed. It appears as though they really try, but the interventions you're using to help them just don't work. You start to wonder if maybe they don't have the right personality types for the tasks you have asked them to complete. You don't want to punish them for something they can't help, and you feel stuck.

Breakdowns in communication are the biggest indicator of a Role Alignment diagnosis. You may notice that your employees don't seem to feel energized by the work they are doing. Achieving goals and desired outcomes doesn't seem to make them feel excited and proud; they're working just to work, not to reach goals.

Possible Interventions: Assess your team with a tool like DiSC®,[14] the Myers-Briggs Type Indicator, the Clifton-Strengths assessment, the Riso-Hudson Enneagram Type Indicator (RHETI®), or Sally Hogshead's Fascinate® test. Work to try and understand what motivates your team, how they communicate, and what gives them energy. When you have a deeper understanding of the people working with you, you can start to match up their skill sets with the tasks needed to complete the job. In the FTN QuickStart,[15] you will find a Matching Tasks to Talents worksheet from our Systemizer School[16] that will help you match your team's talents to their tasks.

TREATMENT PLAN:
Role Alignment

1. **Presenting Problem:** Recently, Joe shadowed each department in his practice. What he found was gut-wrenching. The processes he established early on are now so skewed that they are barely recognizable. Over time, his team individually adapted the steps, and now there is no consistency. Even worse, many of the important key performance indicators (KPIs) were missed completely. His office manager, who was supposed to track incoming referrals and the number of scheduled appointments and troubleshoot any barriers, currently spends all of her time on tasks that do not move the department toward its goal of profitability.

---

[14] If you need a kickass guide to take your team through this process, I recommend Lisa Crilley Mallis of Impactive Strategies. She is a Wiley DiSC® Authorized Partner, and she taught my team everything they know! https://www.impactives-trategies.com

[15] https://www.kaseycompton.com/ftn

[16] https://www.mindsightpartners.com/systemizer-school

2. **Diagnosis:** Role Alignment

3. **Strengths:** Joe is open to change and willing to make tough decisions if necessary.

4. **Baseline:** After spending two weeks with his office manager, Joe determines that the structure necessary for the position is not aligned with her talents. She enjoys social interaction with the staff and engaging in local community events. She thrives when planning events and activities that involve people. She is not disciplined enough to follow a daily routine, and has a hard time seeing the big picture of all the KPIs and the importance of tracking them. She struggles to connect the dots between the outcomes in her department and those in marketing, billing, and human resources. Joe now knows that, in order to set this employee up for success, he needs to realign her tasks with her talents.

5. **Goal:** Joe will increase the profitability of this department by 10% through the alignment of his office manager's tasks to her talents. He will make any changes necessary to support the goal within 30 days.

6. **Interventions:**

   1. Joe had an opening for a revenue-producing position in the company that doesn't require an advanced degree or professional license. Since his office manager is an extrovert, he assigned her to this role two days per week. In it, she will work directly with clients and bill for those services, and the company will achieve a net profit of approximately $16 per billable hour (approximately 10%).

2. She will spend one day a week on office tasks that she is successful at, and her remaining two days per week will be spent engaging in face-to-face community marketing and recruiting. This will increase the company's visibility in Joe's area, promote community involvement, and enhance the number of quality applicants he receives.

3. With the money he makes from his office manager's two days of billable services, Joe will hire someone who is paid at a lower rate to complete and oversee the tasks that she was once responsible for.

7. **Plan for Progress:** Joe will post an ad for a new office manager whose talents align with the tasks of the position. He will monitor the increased revenue his former office manager is now bringing in and make changes when necessary. Joe will plan to reevaluate the progress one month after his new office manager is hired.

DIAGNOSIS #3:
Outcome Delegation

Question: *Are the people closest to the problem empowered to solve it?*

If your employees are not empowered to solve problems within their own departments, it means you or someone else in your organization is a bottleneck. Empowering employees to speak up requires that you relinquish some control. Your ego must be in check, and you must be ready to hear that the processes you created may not cut it anymore. You must be prepared for feedback and able to listen with an open mind and a willingness to change.

When you empower your employees to speak up and resolve the problems they are closest to, you remove yourself as a bottleneck, meaning that your company can grow at a faster pace and with fewer points of congestion.

Presenting Symptoms: Everything appears to be fine, but you can't help but think things could be better. Usually, when problems present themselves, you notice them before anyone else does, but you find out after the fact that your referral coordinator has a waiting list of 150 patients and the company is experiencing a 50% reduction in productivity. You begin to wonder why you didn't know about this sooner. You give your employees a survey to assess their feelings about the roles they hold in the company. Someone reports that they don't feel comfortable speaking up about problems they see in their department, and you're pretty sure it's your referral coordinator.

Possible Interventions: Send out a survey (located in FTN QuickStart) to all of your staff and ask how empowered they feel to solve problems within their departments. This will provide a baseline where you can begin to create interventions. It's also important to give your staff a framework for independent problem-solving. Oftentimes, our employees have come from jobs where empowerment was discouraged. They were told not to speak up, that it was not their place, that they should just be quiet and do their jobs. We're fighting a battle with past experiences here, and, as owners, we must be aware of that. We need to have regular conversations about when to speak up and how. We must train our direct supervisors to collect feedback and teach them what to do with it. We must also reinforce the behavior we want to see when our employees display the capacity for independent problem-solving.

TREATMENT PLAN:
Outcome Delegation

1. **Presenting Problem:** Mary, a supervisor at Hope & Wellness Center, began her performance reviews (as she did every 90 days) and noticed that her referral coordinator, Jessica, seemed to encounter barriers to scheduling new patients with providers. Jessica had a waiting list of 70, but most of the providers were not even fully booked. She was frustrated each and every time she hit a roadblock, and knew it was affecting her ability to meet her goal, but she never said anything.

2. **Diagnosis:** Outcome Delegation

3. **Strengths:** Mary knows that Jessica is aware of the goal of her position; she understands the expectations, but has not felt empowered enough to speak up and create a catalyst for change.

4. **Baseline:** Jessica is new in her role as a referral coordinator. She came from the restaurant business, and this is her first experience in a professional office setting. Her customer service skills are fantastic, and she has a natural ability to care for patients in the way the company promises. She is empathetic and patient-focused, and believes in the mission, vision, and values of the organization.

5. **Goal:** Should anything get in the way of her reaching her goal, the referral coordinator will communicate the barriers and roadblocks she encounters to her supervisor.

6. **Interventions:**
   1. Mary will help Jessica draft an email that reminds the providers of the policies regarding their schedules and the expectations for booking patients.

2. Jessica will draft canned emails that she can quickly send out to providers as reminders about opening blocks of time, rescheduling client appointments, and making recurring appointments the norm.

3. Jessica will triage the waiting list and get all of the patients scheduled with the providers within the next seven days.

7. **Plan for Progress:** Mary will make a note in Jessica's performance improvement plan and schedule weekly meetings with her. The plan will be revised to ensure that it equips Jessica with the language she needs to accurately communicate problems, the tools she needs to intervene, and access to the support she requires to resolve them.

DIAGNOSIS #4:
Linchpin Redundancy

Question: *Is your practice designed to operate unabated when a critical employee is unavailable?*

All offices have a unicorn, that one employee who can do it all—the one everyone comes to when there's a problem, the one who helps resolve issues on the fly, the one who can fill in for anyone in their absence. This person may look like a unicorn to some, but to me, they're a bottleneck. This key employee holds everything together, and that's actually NOT a good thing. As a business owner, I find it quite terrifying. You must work to create a practice that is designed to operate as usual when any employee is unavailable. We get comfortable with routine. We move along, day after day, because everything seems to work—until life happens and it doesn't.

One thing I know very little about is billing. Once upon a time, I had a billing department that was run by and relied solely on a single individual. This person knew all the passwords for all the accounts, how all the electronic remittance advices worked, how to post the payments, which reports to run and when to run them, and the processes for mailing statements and billing secondary claims. You name it, she knew it. There was no reason for anyone else to know all those things, right? Wrong!

Denials came in left and right, and we had no idea why. I relied solely on her experience and expertise to solve these problems because I was no help. Check after check for zero dollars came in, and the aging schedule grew and grew. Before I knew it, there was over $300,000 outstanding and I had no idea how I was going to make payroll. It was bad, but at least my billing department employee was there and helping—until life happened.

When her life took a different turn, she was unable to fulfill the tasks she was hired to do. It was all on me, and I felt like I had let my team down. Not because I didn't know how to do billing, but because I had left the viability of our entire billing department in the hands of one individual, and now she was gone. I had been ill-prepared and reckless, and I was paying for it.

Presenting Symptoms: When critical employees leave, their absence is felt by all. If they are out for a day, or two, or even a weeklong vacation, others feel lost. During their absence, other staff members may need to call them because there's an important question they don't know how to answer. Other processes may come to halt because no one knows the steps in order to complete the task. Maybe you hear someone say, "It can wait until she gets back," but waiting creates a bottleneck you cannot afford.

Possible Interventions: Plan for these absences by making sure you have accessible training videos and standard operating procedures (SOPs) for all the systems and processes in every department. Once that is completed, engage in the Swapping Staff activity (found in FTN QuickStart). Ensure that every job can be covered by another person in the company, and at the same level of expected quality. Set a goal for this and ensure that every individual is cross-trained. Set an incentive for those who have a thorough SOP for their department. SOPs must be clear enough that when staff swap roles, their jobs can be executed without input.

TREATMENT PLAN:
Linchpin Redundancy

1. **Presenting Problem:** The goal for Jerry's practice over the past month was to streamline systems. A part of that process was to ensure that each person's position could be covered if they were out of the office for two days or more. Jerry hadn't started systemizing yet, but he knew it was necessary because of the breakdown in productivity that occurred when several employees were absent over the last two months. Great ideas were sparked, actions were taken, but no one ever followed through on them. Worse than that, there was no accountability system in place for the people who were responsible for each project.
2. **Diagnosis:** Linchpin Redundancy
3. **Strengths:** Jerry recognizes that there is a problem, and so does the rest of his team.
4. **Baseline:** Nothing is getting done, and what little is getting done isn't done well.

5. **Goal:** Within the next 12 weeks, the team will be cross-trained and able to perform each other's jobs for at least two weeks without sacrificing quality.

6. **Interventions:**

   1. Each employee will begin to document the steps to complete each process that their position is responsible for (for example: completing payroll, resubmitting a denied claim, or taking a new referral). They will document as much of their position as possible in preparation for cross-training.

   2. The team will participate in an activity called Swap Seats, in which they each learn one new position by using each other's SOPs to complete the job.

   3. Each staff member will make a list of all the questions they still have about the new position while they attempt to work in it. Based on feedback from the swap, each person responsible for a role will make changes to their SOP when they return to their position.

   4. This process will continue until each position in the company can be performed by someone else.

7. **Plan for Progress:** The team will meet on a weekly basis to discuss progress made so far and make adjustments if necessary. By the end of the 12 weeks, each position should have a fully functioning SOP and each role should have at least two people who can effectively cover it.

DIAGNOSIS #5:
Problem-Solving Solutions

Question: *Do you and your team have an effective working model for solving problems as they arise?*

My team and I at Mindsight Behavioral Group developed the PASS Method™ during the onset of the global pandemic of 2020. As a group, we communicated twice daily while performing our jobs from home. At this time, we not only had to face regular business problems, but also knew that we stood to face many more due to COVID-19. In this situation, I came to the realization that my team needed guidance in the problem-solving department. Most entrepreneurs pride themselves on problem-solving; after all, this is what we do every single day of our lives. What I noticed was, not all of my employees had that same ability—and if they did, they were holding out on me. During Zoom meeting after Zoom meeting, I sat and watched the frustration grow on their faces. An issue would arise, and it would look something like this.

"Our numbers are dropping," said Jackie, the self-proclaimed Resident Genius on our team. (She's really our billing manager, but I let her call herself whatever makes her feel good. So, Resident Genius it is.)

"If the providers continue at this pace for three months, we will have to cut support staff. There won't be enough revenue to cover their payroll," I jumped in.

"While I cover the front desk, I get several callers that hang up when I answer," someone else chimed in.

"Yeah, the other day I talked to the providers via email and phone constantly. They all had questions and wanted to know what the plan was for tele-working," said another.

"Maybe we could put up a billboard!" another person exclaimed. I clenched my teeth. This meeting was going nowhere fast. Can you see what I was seeing? There was no focus, no direction, and no goal. Jackie initiated the conversation when she identified a problem. Instead of working together to quickly formulate a solution, each person started to point out all of their own problems, which caused a heightened level of anxiety and stress. After one hour, we were no further along than when we started. All we knew was that there were lots of problems, and we had no plan to fix them.

At this moment, I realized that I needed to give my team a process for solving problems, one that they could utilize without me. It became known as the PASS Method™, and the outline and examples can be found in your FTN QuickStart. Now, before you keep reading and start to feel anxiety because you don't know what the method is, or think, "I don't have time to learn something new," just take a moment and breathe. This method is simply one that works for me and my practice. If you already have a way to solve problems that you can teach to your team, then please use that! My method is there for you if you need it, and if you don't, that's fine too. The point here is to have a predictable way to solve problems so that your team can stay focused and be efficient in the use of their time.

Presenting Symptoms: You find yourself in situations much like mine above. You leave staff meetings, team meetings, or administrative meetings feeling like they were pointless, a waste of time. Rather than getting problems solved, more problems get pointed out. There is a lack of focus within the department and within the organization overall. People appear to be "doing" without a clear understanding of what that "doing" is going to get them. Interventions applied to identified problems are not being followed through on, and there's no accountability for those to whom they're assigned.

Possible Interventions: Implement a problem-solving process such as the PASS Method™ with your team. Teach them the way you want problems to be solved and provide them with a guide that will not only support them, but hold them accountable as well. Have them each turn in a worksheet to you that regularly outlines their progress. Make sure that one employee is identified as the person accountable for the tasks the team has been assigned. Put all of these worksheets in one place, whether it be on a shared folder in the Google Drive or in an accessible hardcover binder somewhere in your office. Encourage the team to reference them in future meetings when the problems identified are similar to those solved in the past.

TREATMENT PLAN:
Problem-solving Solutions

1. **Presenting Problem:** Jackie said the practice would be in trouble if productivity didn't increase. The providers reduced their hours of availability because they didn't have childcare or couldn't work from home.

2. **Diagnosis:** Problem-solving Solutions

3. **Strengths:** Jackie's team is full of natural-born problem-solvers. She is focused and determined to overcome any roadblocks to productivity and profitability.

4. **Baseline:** The current productivity numbers decreased by 30%. If the company didn't increase its productivity by at least 15%, the revenue would not support the current number of support staff, and someone would lose their job.

5. **Goal:** Productivity will increase by a minimum of 15% within the next 30 days.

6. **Interventions:**

   1. Jackie will use the PASS Method™ for problem- solving to help her team stay focused and efficient. (An outline of how to use the PASS Method™ and Jackie's PASS are located in FTN QuickStart.)

   2. The team will create a comprehensive package of three possible solutions. First, they will create a text-to-talk campaign. To increase the ease of self-referral, they will design a simple, highly shareable logo that reads, "Text CARE2020 to 474747 to Speak to a Counselor."

   3. The logo will be placed on virtual flyers that will be sent to all referral sources and circulated throughout all social media platforms.

   4. The team will encourage the referral sources to direct their patients to "Text CARE2020 to 474747" for any mental health concerns, screenings, or questions. This is quick and easy to remember and doesn't require passing anything from hand to hand.

   5. Additional flyers with QR codes will be offered to any community partner who is interested in having them in their facility.

7. **Plan for Progress:** Progress will be tracked by weekly evaluation of insights from social media platforms and through our referral tracker, which calculates all new leads. The marketing coordinator will be responsible for creating the campaigns, the logo, and the flyers, and the client care coordinator will be responsible for tracking leads as they come in. The team will meet every morning for 15 minutes to call out the number of engagements and

new referrals from the previous day. Adjustments will be made as necessary, based on what is and isn't working.

DON'T BE A CLYDESDALE

Our businesses never have a shortage of needs, and the method with which we try and address them is often nonexistent. When we don't know where to start, we just start.

When we lack the tools needed to move our business forward, we end up doing a lot of *doing. Doing* more work than necessary. *Doing* more tasks that aren't making our business any more profit. *Doing* more systemizing to improve processes that will in no way impact the bottom line. We work our tails off *doing*, but we're totally missing the point. *Doing* isn't going to get us what we want. It's just going to make us tired, burned out, and resentful. We wear our workaholic badge of pride and believe the lie that killing ourselves must mean we're on the right track.

Chris is a mental health professional in the beautiful state of Colorado. Like many of us, he started his career at a community mental health center. His passion for helping people, coupled with his relentless work ethic, made him a standout. As he began to grow in his career, he received many accolades. Regular pats on the back for his enthusiasm, his attention to detail, and his ability to leave no stone unturned made him feel good. Chris became a workaholic, the company's own Clydesdale. Before he knew it, his identity was measured by how much work he produced, how much progress he made, and how many billable hours he could generate. He sought out validation for his continued efforts until he overworked his body and tapped out his mind. When the Clydesdale pulled too many carriages, didn't take enough time to rest, and kept pushing despite exhaustion, it began to break down.

Imagine being known as the workhorse. When Chris couldn't work at that same pace any longer, he felt lost. The badge that once contributed to his sense of pride now made him feel like an imposter. He had to slow down. He had to forgo that "workaholic" title and adopt a new one, but what would it be? What would ever give him the same satisfaction as being needed by everyone? He started his job in community mental health to help people. He was on a mission to make an impact in the lives of others. But because of the industry's demands, productivity goals, picking up the slack for those not as Clydesdale-ish, and the need to stay relevant to maintain employment, Chris had compromised his initial sense of purpose in order to perform.

Now, just to be clear, Chris was working as an employee, not an entrepreneur. He was playing someone else's game by someone else's rules. He wasn't always able to do the most impactful thing because there were times that that was not what management wanted. He didn't have that compass in his back pocket, and despite all of his efforts to impart his opinion in the corporate world, he was unsuccessful. Chris was left feeling as though he only had two choices: One, he could succumb to the expectations of his employer, forgoing his purpose of helping people to satisfy the company's productivity expectations. Or, two, he could recognize the fact that he had something special—he had the ability to stay true to who he wanted to be while meeting the goal of any business (perhaps his own): profitability.

Chris needed a change of pace. That ultimately came when he made the decision to go out on his own as a healthcare entrepreneur. He had the business acumen to know that he had to be profitable, and he had the heart to do it with purpose. Now, Chris manages his own private practice, writes books, and has a membership community for others who can identify with his journey. I can't help but wonder what he will do now that he has a compass, now that he knows what it takes to achieve balance. Will he use the HHN to help him understand exactly what to do in order to make the biggest impact in his business? Has he officially traded in that workhorse title for something better, something that won't be a hindrance to his health, something that will allow him to make money and pursue his purpose? Knowing what I know of Chris, I would say yes to all of the above.

You don't have to be a Clydesdale; you don't have to go through what Chris went through. All you need to know is that when you use a tool like the HHN to pinpoint your practice's diagnosis, you will always be moving in the right direction. You will be able to achieve order *and* confidence and, best of all, you'll be able to live the life you always wanted to live.

Chapter Six
Treatment Plan for Your Biz

"My instincts got me into this mess, and a plan will get me out."

That was me, giving myself a pep talk back in Chapter One, when I nearly lost it all—my sanity, my pride, and my business. My Thanksgiving story is quite a common cautionary tale. Although you may not have been eating turkey while your business fell apart, you've likely experienced something similar. Relying on your gut to make decisions, looking for the goosebumps on your arms to tell you it's time to slow down, or employing all your friends because they're so wonderful always gets you into trouble. After all, you can't run your business on feelings, no matter how badly you might want to.

When my near-business-death experience struck back in 2017, there was no such thing as an FTN methodology for addressing a business's problems—but man, I wish there had been. Although I didn't whip out the book, turn to Chapter Two, and start diagnosing, I did go back to what I knew, which was how to treat my clients. I asked myself what my personal strengths were, what my business was doing well, and what it needed to do better. I designed a plan that gave me hope in the toughest of situations, one that helped rally what was left of my troops and made them feel confident that the captain of their ship had a plan and was prepared to chart the course. It was not perfect, but it got the job done. It helped me stay focused and reach my goal of getting my finances in order so that I could make decisions based on numbers.

Going through the toughest of situations allowed me to slow down enough for my entrepreneurial confidence to find me. It wasn't until I took chance after chance and made a few mistakes along the way that I was able to believe it was all going to be okay. Sometimes we just need to slow down, look around, and take a deep breath. A treatment plan is more than just a plan; it allows you to pause and think. It reduces uncertainty. It's the antithesis of insecurity. It's what you needed yesterday, what you need tomorrow, and what you need right now.

In this chapter, I will teach you all of the necessary components to create a treatment plan for your practice, one that will allow you to level up without any wasted time, energy, or effort. You can do this. You *will* do this because, as a healthcare entrepreneur, you're better suited for it than anyone!

DESIGN THE TREATMENT PLAN

Every good treatment plan starts with a presenting problem, a diagnosis, a baseline, strengths, a clear goal, carefully designed interventions, and a plan for progress. This is how a provider can focus on the problem at hand so the patient is best served. As I'm sure you recall, back in Chapter Two, we discussed using the HHN as the tool to determine your business's diagnosis. With the supporting information from the chapters focused on **SALES**, **PROFIT**, and **ORDER**, you are now ready to use that diagnosis and create your treatment plan.

PRESENTING PROBLEM

What has led to the diagnosis? You already know your business's diagnosis from the HHN, but here you want to describe the problem. How is this problem affecting your practice's ability to function and work toward profitability?

DIAGNOSIS

To determine your business's diagnosis, take the HHN Assessment and identify the lowest unmet Core Need on the lowest foundational level. This becomes your diagnosis, and the focus of your treatment until the need is satisfied.

BASELINE

You've had headaches every day for the last three weeks. You're not quite sure, but you think a good number of them are migraines. This isn't something you've dealt with before, other than a short stint back in high school. You decide that these headaches are starting to impact your quality of life, so you schedule an appointment with your primary care physician. After another week has passed, you go in and sit down on the exam table. The doctor asks you what's wrong and you begin to explain your symptoms. You tell her that your head hurts every single day, and some days it hurts so badly you have to lie down in a dark room just to get any relief.

What does the doctor do? Does she whip out the prescription pad and scribble the name of a pill that is sure to solve your problem? No! She asks clarifying questions so that she can create a baseline.

"At what point in the day do the headaches occur? What happens right before they start? How long do they last? What gives you relief? Has this ever happened to you before? If so, what did you do? Have you ever taken medication to treat the problem?" she will mostly likely ask.

Does this sound familiar? These are all common questions used to create a baseline. A doctor cannot start treatment interventions before a baseline is in place because, without it, there would be nothing with which to compare a patient's progress.

When you come back for your follow-up appointment in two weeks, your doctor will ask you about your symptoms again and record your results. Hopefully, by that time, you will have a reduction of symptoms—and she will know that because she has written down a baseline in your chart.

Without a baseline, you have nothing with which to compare the results and effectiveness of your interventions. You can gather baseline data from a long laundry list of sources that you will find below. Just know: This is a critical part of your treatment plan. The following information is a resource to serve as a starting point as you seek out and gather the necessary information to include in your treatment plan.

SALES
Starting Points for Collecting Baseline Information

1. **Lifestyle Congruence:** *Do you know what your practice's sales (billable sessions) must be in order to support your personal financial comfort level?*
   - Aging reports (accounts receivable)
   - Productivity reports
   - Owner's compensation
   - Your Profit First allocations (if you choose to use this system)
   - Profit & Loss statement
   - Balance sheet

2. **Prospect and Provider Attraction:** *Do you attract enough clients to support your level of needed sales for a profitable practice (20% net profit or higher), and do you attract enough providers to support the patient demand?*
   - Employee turnover rates
   - Application and hiring statistics
   - Profit & Loss statement

- Metrics on employees hired in a calendar year versus employees on payroll at the end of that calendar year
- Indeed's hiring dashboard and features can give you statistics on the number of applicants and how many prospects you are attracting
- Social media insights
- Intake funnel dashboard
- Provider productivity reports

3. **Client Conversion:** *Do you convert enough of the right clients to support your level of needed sales?*
   - Intake data
     ▷ Number of calls versus number of appointments booked
     ▷ New clients booked daily
     ▷ Reasons for not booking
     ▷ Stats on where your clients are hearing about you
     ▷ Sources of leads
   - Marketing trends
   - Website analytics that show bounce rates, time spent onsite, opt-in numbers, and statistics

4. **Delivering on Commitments:** *Do you fully deliver on your commitments to your clients?*
   - Message matchup
   - Waiting list analysis
   - Appointments that coincide with treatment plan recommendations
   - Successfully discharged patients
   - Retention rates of providers
   - Follow-up after first session report

- Urgency of scheduling
- Number of patients you have referred to other practices

5. **Collecting on Commitments:** *Do your clients fully deliver on their commitments to you?*
   - Aging reports (accounts receivable)
   - Client balances
   - No-show and late-cancel statistics

PROFIT
Starting Points for Collecting Baseline Information

1. **Debt Eradication:** *Do you consistently remove debt rather than accumulate it?*
   - Monthly statements
   - Profit & Loss statement
   - Balance sheet
   - Credit card statements and balances
   - Mortgage statements with interest rates

2. **Margin Health:** *Does each of your offerings have a healthy profit margin, and do you continually seek ways to improve these margins?*
   - Profit & Loss statement
   - Reimbursement rates versus provider pay
   - Calendar of your efforts to negotiate rate increases

3. **Appointment Frequency:** *Do your clients repeatedly and regularly schedule with you as recommended in their treatment plans?*
   - Intake data
     ▹ Number of calls versus number of appointments booked
     ▹ New clients booked daily

> ▷ Reasons for not booking
>
> ▷ Follow-up appointments booked by providers

4. **Profitable Leverage:** *When debt is used, is it used to generate predictable, increased profitability?*
   - Profit & Loss statement
   - Cost analysis
   - Return on investment (ROI) analysis
   - Break-even analysis

5. **Cash Reserves:** *Does your practice have enough cash reserves to cover all expenses for three months or longer?*
   - Bank statements
   - Profit First allocations
   - Balance sheet

ORDER
Starting Points for Collecting Baseline Information

1. **Systemization:** *Do you have an ongoing, working model to reduce bottlenecks, congestion points, and inefficiencies?*
   - Identifying Bottlenecks Worksheet (in FTN QuickStart)
   - Set goals for the time a process should take
   - Check for bottlenecks regularly

2. **Role Alignment:** *Are people's roles and responsibilities matched with their talents?*
   - Matching Tasks to Talents Worksheet (in FTN QuickStart)

3. **Outcome Delegation:** *Do the people closest to the problem feel empowered to resolve it?*
   - Staff Survey (in FTN QuickStart)

4. **Linchpin Redundancy:** *Is your practice designed to operate unabated when critical employees are unavailable?*

- Swapping Roles Worksheet (in FTN QuickStart)
- Standard operating procedures

5. **Problem-solving Solutions:** *Do you and your team have an effective working model for solving problems as they arise?*
   - PASS Method™ (in FTN QuickStart)

STRENGTHS

You do *you*. Always focus on your strengths. I told you I was going to show you how to do this. This is me showing you how to do this. Find the things you're naturally good at, things you enjoy, and amplify them. Most healthcare entrepreneurs don't even realize how they can use their strengths to their advantage as they design interventions. Your strengths make you different, and different makes interventions effective. Consider choosing your interventions from a strengths-based perspective. In other words, choose interventions that are aligned with what you naturally do well. When you do this, you will find less resistance to the ways you choose to fix your practice—and more success.

GOALS

Goals are the *whats*. When you use the HHN as an assessment tool to determine your business's diagnosis, you create your goals at the same time. The question that corresponds to the Core Need will be restated to create your goal. For example, if your diagnosis is Cash Reserves, you will have asked yourself this question: *Does your practice have enough cash reserves to cover three months of expenses?* Knowing what that three months of expenses is, your goal will look something like this: "Mindsight Behavioral Group will have $245,000 in cash reserves in order to cover three months' worth of expenses." Simply put, the goal on your treatment plan is always a restatement of the question that led you to the diagnosis.

INTERVENTIONS

Interventions are the *hows.* The interventions are where you leverage your strengths to create action steps that will elicit change. What's it going to take in order to reach your goal? It's important to note that there's no way I could possibly tell you exactly how to fix every single problem in your practice. I wish I could, but there are so many variables that make that practically impossible. When designing interventions, choose no more than three for any goal. You must choose the ones that are most directly related to the goal, and most likely to make an impact. The reason you want to keep the interventions to a minimum is, you need to be able to easily tell which one works. If there are too many running at one time, that will be extremely hard to do.

PLAN FOR PROGRESS

The plan is the *whens.* The plan for progress not only puts a timestamp on our project, it also holds us accountable through deadlines and contingency plans. In the plan, you will note the frequency of your measurement of progress as well as the secondary actions you plan to take if the first set of interventions is unsuccessful. Your plan for progress will include:

1. The person accountable for the intervention.
2. The frequency of the intervention and/or the frequency of its evaluation.
3. The intensity of the intervention and/or the intensity of its evaluation.

FTN TX PLAN IN ACTION: ERNESTINA'S TREATMENT PLAN

Ernestina is a practice owner in the heart of a Latinx community in Chicago. At this time, it's just her and one other provider, but she wants to grow and have a larger group of professionals to serve her ideal Latinx client. Her phone is ringing, but she knows it will have to ring a lot more in order for her to hire more clinicians. She also knows that she doesn't want to keep taking new clients because her time needs to be spent working *on* the business rather than *in* it.

Right now, she needs money more than she needs time. Her call log shows that she's receiving approximately three calls per day and scheduling two appointments per week for new clients—about a 13% conversion rate. When she takes the HHN assessment, she scores a no in both Prospect and Provider Attraction and Client Conversion. Since Prospect and Provider Attraction has a lower number assigned in the foundational level of **SALES**, she starts there.

Presenting Problem: Ernestina needs to make sure that her current providers have a full caseload and generate their target number of billable sessions for the practice.

Diagnosis: Prospect Attraction

Strengths: Ernestina already has a dashboard to track KPIs that she pulled from the resource library in her membership community, Mindsight Partners,[17] and does a great job at interpreting data.

Baseline: Her call log shows that she receives approximately three calls per day and schedules two appointments per week for new clients. Her new clients heard about her through a

---

[17] Mindsight Partners—Expert-Led Membership Community: https://www.mindsightpartners.com

commonly used platform in her area. She pays a fee for the use of the platform, and the platform sends referrals to her.

According to the information, it appears that Ernestina does not attract enough clients to fill the schedules of the providers in her practice. Since she wants to grow the business and hire more therapists, she needs more referrals in order to feel good about that decision.

Goal: The practice will attract 10 new leads per day to support the practice's level of needed sales for profitability (30% net profit) within the next 30 days.

With the current conversion rate of 13%, this would mean that 6.5 leads would convert to clients on a weekly basis. Since Ernestina already determined that 500 billable sessions per month and six new clients per week would satisfy her Lifestyle Congruence, she now has a measurable and attainable goal.

Setting a goal that is not measurable or attainable will set you up for a great deal of frustration and disappointment. Ernestina's goal is simple and measurable because she wants 10 new leads daily. It's attainable because she will implement a marketing intervention, which we'll talk more about in the next chapter, to get more calls on a regular basis.

Interventions:

1. Further define Latinx to expand her messaging and reach.

2. Create reaction videos such as TikToks, psychoeducational material, and promos that are in both English and Spanish. The goal is for these videos is to reach a large number of people in the Latinx community.

Plan for Progress: Once the videos are created and shared on all social media platforms, Ernestina will watch the insights and statistics weekly to determine which type of video is getting the most engagement. Once that is determined, she will create more of that specific category of video and reach an even wider audience. If none of the videos produce new leads, she will implement different interventions within 30 days.

Ernestina went with a slightly different approach to get new leads, something a little less traditional. She decided to use her strengths to her benefit and created novelas on Tik-Tok that got tons—and I mean tons—of attention! Ernestina's target audience latched on her concept and embraced the fact that she was speaking directly to them. Her local community caught on to all the hype and she began to get more than 10 new leads daily. Pretty soon, her phone was blowing up. She had to hire three virtual assistants and a total of five therapists. Her practice is still growing due to the traction she gained from her first set of interventions. She's on a roll and out to take over the Latinx world!

Even though you may only be working to address one diagnosis at a time, you may have several goals in place and even more interventions. The beauty of this system is that, once you're focused on the right problem at the right time, good things happen. No more wasting time and energy, or getting caught up in the survival trap.

FTN TX PLAN IN ACTION: HEATHER'S TREATMENT PLAN

Let's try another example of a goal that had great success! In 2020, the great state of Massachusetts had a population of approximately 6.7 million people, and my friend Heather only needed a few of them to ring her practice's line each day. She needed even fewer to convert into clients. Heather's practice was doing well, but she knew it could be better. It had so much potential, but she got hung up in the day-to-day operations. She was about to lose sight of the practice's goal of profitability.

In Heather's words, she was her own biggest bottleneck. She received lots of calls, emails, and texts from new leads, but many of them wanted to use insurance that she didn't accept, and another large portion seemed to fall through the cracks at some point during their journey.

Heather said, "They look good on paper and sound optimistic on the phone, but when they are sent the consent forms and other paperwork required before their first appointment, we often never hear from them again. And they definitely didn't make it to their first appointment. We are losing money."

Presenting Problem: Heather is not converting enough of the leads generated through her website. The clients are overwhelmed and don't follow through with the process.

Diagnosis: Client Conversion

Strengths: Heather manages her own website, so it will be easy for her to make changes as needed. She also has a solid understanding of the client journey and the point at which they appear to be opting out.

Baseline: Heather has a dashboard for tracking incoming calls and conversions. Based on that information, she learned that her current conversion rate is 50%, which she thinks is low, especially since she accepts many of the kinds of insurance that people in her area have. The dashboard also indicates that the majority of her clients are finding her through her website. And she knows that the drop-off point is when the client is sent paperwork prior to their first appointment. After taking a quick look at her website and talking to other entrepreneurs in the same industry, she has a pretty good idea what the problem is.

Goal: The practice will convert enough of the right clients and increase its conversion rate from 50% to 75% in the next 45 days.

Interventions:

1. Heather will narrow her sales funnel to attract more of the right type of client to her practice. She will state clearly on her website what kinds of insurance she accepts so that there is no confusion.

2. Heather will improve the client journey by streamlining the process. She will look for all points where the client exits the funnel and apply "fixes." Heather will manage clients' expectations from the beginning of their journey, so they know what the process looks like from the start.

Plan for Progress: Heather will monitor the new client leads and her conversion rate closely, on a weekly basis. She will allow one month for the funnel and client journey interventions. If there are no significant changes within 30 days, Heather will begin retargeting her clients through Google Ads and modify her script for leads coming through on the phone.

Heather thinks the new clients are overwhelmed. They are highly qualified leads, have already had an interaction with her client care coordinator, and the practice knows they are a good fit. The reason the majority of these new clients have reached out is because they're overwhelmed by life and struggling with anxiety and symptoms of depression. Heather thinks there's a good chance that the intake process is too stressful, and they're finding an easy reason to opt out.

Heather knows that narrowing the top of her intake funnel to attract more qualified leads will help her reach her goal. Clients will feel less overwhelmed and will know what to expect. She wants to take every opportunity to get the best return on her investment. She wants to ensure that her funnel is designed so that at least 75% of the leads that enter it convert to new clients.

How will she do that? Heather will apply interventions that best meet the needs of her goals and objectives. Since those are now clear, she can focus much more closely on designing the interventions that will make a significant impact in her practice. Remember, even the greatest interventions will prove useless if the diagnosis is wrong and the goals are unclear.

Heather also has a clear plan with an end date. She knows that if her goal is not met within the 30-day window, her next step is to modify the interventions as already determined in her treatment plan. This plan not only holds Heather accountable, but also puts her on track for measurable success.

STAY FOCUSED ON THE GOAL

If I were to go out on a limb here, I would bet you've never written a treatment plan for your practice, but have written thousands for your patients. I'd say that when you recognize you have a problem and decide to do something about it, you may stick a few Post-It-Notes in places throughout your office and, because you're so busy, rarely give them a second glance. I'm not judging; I did the same thing. I'm notorious for writing things in notebooks and then losing them.

Maybe you like the idea of a system and the idea of organization, but you lack the follow-through to get it done. This is precisely why you must go online and download my FTN Workbook, which can be found in FTN QuickStart.[18] You must print it out, three-hole punch it, stick it in a binder, and hold yourself to it. When you consistently diagnose and treat your practice with a written plan, you will start to gain traction. You will set goals and achieve them just as quickly as you write out the interventions. You'll gain momentum and feel so much more confident in your ability to run your practice.

In the next chapter, I will cover interventions for your treatment plan in even more detail. These are the common fixes for each of the potential diagnoses your business may have. It's one thing to be able to identify a problem, but when you're equipped with the tools to fix it, that's even better.

---

[18] https://www.kaseycompton.com/ftn

Chapter Seven

Design Interventions

THERE'S NOTHING BETTER THAN WALKING INTO THE OFFICE first thing Monday morning and hearing the words, "We need to talk." To top it all off, they're coming from the mouth of my billing manager, and I never hear from her unless things are really bad or she smells a donut.

"It must be bad. Nothing good ever comes of those four words," I say. But I'm kind of lying. And Jackie kind of is, too. We both secretly like a problem, because we like a challenge.

I know she has discovered an issue because I can hear it in the tone of her voice, and she can't look me in the eye.

"Okay, so here's what I found this morning. All the claims from one payer have been denied…" she starts.

When she says "denied," I immediately know we have a Collecting on Commitments diagnosis, right there in our **SALES** level; before I even realize what I'm doing, I diagnose my business. I know that if our claims are denied, our aging reports are also up. The goal of the billing department is to have 0% of revenue outstanding past 60 days, and this is definitely going to disrupt that. Our baseline has to be bad. If all the claims from one payer are being denied, I guesstimate at least 25% of all revenue is withheld.

My next thought is about interventions. Since I'm not a biller, I pretty much just focus on the goal and let Jackie handle the rest.

"What's the plan?" I ask, knowing she already has one.

"I think I know what the problem is. I've been on the phone all morning and I believe there is an issue with the clearinghouse. I can wait for the other claims to formally deny, because I know they will, and then I can submit directly to the payer for a faster remit."

"Is that efficient?" I inquire. Remember, I'm not a biller, so all I have to go on is *does it work*, and *how much will it cost*?

"Well, not really," Jackie admits. "But if we don't do it this way for now, we have to wait for the formal denial, then try to submit through the clearinghouse again, taking the chance that the issue still hasn't been corrected on the payer's part."

"So, basically we have to spend more time on the front end to ensure we get the money before the next payroll?"

"Exactly. As soon as I resubmit, I will focus all my energy on correcting the clearinghouse issue so this won't happen again. The next batch we submit will be paid."

I hope she's right, and fortunately for the both of us, she usually is. In case you need a translation, like I did, this is Jackie's problem, and this is Jackie's plan.

Problem: Our claims are denied because there is a problem with the clearinghouse that is out of our control: When we submit claims electronically, an important modifier is left off the claim, which causes the denial.

Plan: Although it's much more efficient to go through the clearinghouse built into the Electronic Health Records (EHR), if we do so, the claims will still be denied—at least until the clearinghouse fixes its internal problem. Since we need the money to come in quickly, we have to bypass the EHR altogether and bill the claims directly from the payer's website. This makes things much more difficult, because they will then have to be reconciled within the EHR once paid—but at least they will be paid. When the clearinghouse is fixed, we will go back to billing the claims as we normally do.

The interventions, or the fixes, for our practice's problems are one of my favorite parts of being an entrepreneur, and I hope they will be for you too. Interventions are things you're already doing. In fact, you're probably doing more of this component of the treatment plan than you are anything else. These are the actions that make us feel like we're moving closer to our goal. And we actually would be if we were applying the right interventions to the right diagnosis at the right time. But we're not.

Interventions are consuming our to-do lists. Whether it's running a social media ad campaign or putting together 100 Halloween goodie bags for our community partners to increase referrals, we do things to drive more leads, create more profit, or increase efficiency; these are all considered interventions. Perhaps you decide to swap the roles of your receptionist and client care coordinator to better align their tasks to talents. You could even run an audit on year-to-date expenses and look for ways to cut them by 10%. These are all interventions you use in your practice every single day without even knowing it.

Jackie came to me about her billing problem, but not because she needed me to solve it. She already knew how to do that. She wanted to let me know because she understands that her department does not operate in isolation. She knows that all departments impact one another and wanted reassurance that compromising efficiency was okay for now. Whether she came to me directly or to a fellow department manager, she was screening to ensure that no other diagnoses were present that would impact hers. She looked for validation that her timing was right, that her idea was on point, and that there was nothing else she needed to consider. Like Jackie, you just need to design the interventions at the right time, for the right diagnosis.

INTERVENTIONS ARE THE HOWS

Interventions are the *hows*. They are how you will meet your goal and address your practice's diagnosis. Remember Ernestina, who struggled to get enough clients to meet her practice's productivity needs? I already told you that her interventions worked, her goal was met, and the Core Need was satisfied. What I didn't tell you was why they worked. Let's look at Ernestina's Treatment Plan again.

ERNESTINA'S TREATMENT PLAN

Presenting Problem: Ernestina needs to make sure her current providers have a full caseload and generate their target number of billable sessions for the practice.

Diagnosis: Prospect Attraction

Strengths: Ernestina has a dashboard to track KPIs and does a great job at interpreting data. She also has a very close relationship with her town and strong ties to the Latinx community.

Baseline: Her call log shows that she receives approximately three calls per day and schedules two appointments per week for new clients. Her new clients heard about her through a commonly used marketing platform in her area. She pays a fee for the use of the platform, which sends referrals to her.

Goal: The practice will attract 10 new leads per day to support its level of needed sales for a profitable practice within the next 30 days.

Interventions:

1. Ernestina will create an email marketing campaign to send to all of her referral sources from captured emails.
2. She will put work into the SEO of her website with the help of a trusted company.

3. She will up her social media game by pumping out content that helps people quickly.

4. She will make the process for getting an appointment easy, thinking about the client journey and asking herself, how do most clients prefer to be scheduled? Her approach will accommodate them.

5. She will formulate an email marketing nurture campaign to send to the exported client emails from her EHR system and give them a simple call to action (CTA) so that they can easily get back on the books.

We must ask ourselves if our interventions are intentional and deliberate actions toward reaching our goal. In Ernestina's case, the answer is yes. This is why her interventions worked. They were directly related to the goal, and she measured them based on outcomes.

1. Email marketing campaigns are among the most effective types of marketing, especially if you have a list of subscribers who already know, like, and trust you. If Ernestina creates an email marketing campaign to send to all of her referral sources, serving them this amazing availability, they'll never even think of it as a sell. They'll think of it as what it is—an opportunity. They have patients who need help, and Ernestina works hard to meet their needs.

2. Utilizing the services of an SEO expert will ensure that Ernestina's website is seen by her ideal client. This means that any leads generated will be right for her practice, thereby increasing her conversion percentage.

3. By taking the same messaging and aesthetic from her website, she will be able to create more social media content for the Latinx community. Here, they will absorb quick tips for mental health, giving them a quick win.

4. If Ernestina goes back to her newly designed website and ensures that the client journey is clear and seamless, she will have a much more successful outcome. She doesn't want any confused clients! She needs to look for clear calls to action and well-defined expectations throughout the site.

5. Lastly, if Ernestina goes back to her EHR system and exports the client names and email addresses she has collected since her practice started back in 2018, she can easily import them into an email marketing platform. Then she can send out a nurture campaign designed to provide previous clients with strategies for maintaining mental wellness and give them an easy way to reach back out if they come to a point where they need support again. This campaign will be simple, thoughtful, and helpful for past clients, especially because it will outline the new set of openings with providers. She will make it easy for them to schedule with a simple call-to-action button in the email. She will keep in mind that they may need to speak to her client care coordinator first, which is no problem, because she will provide a link for that. She will make it easy. The simpler something is, the more likely a client is to follow through. Give them as few opportunities as possible to change their mind.

Let's look at Heather's Treatment Plan again. This time, we'll expand on the interventions designed to meet the goal.

HEATHER'S TREATMENT PLAN

Presenting Problem: Heather is not converting enough of the leads generated through her website. The clients are over-whelmed and don't follow through with the process.

Diagnosis: Client Conversion

Strengths: Heather manages her own website, so it will be easy for her to make changes as needed. She also has a solid understanding of the client journey and the point at which they appear to be opting out.

Baseline: Heather has a dashboard for tracking incoming calls and conversion. Based on that information, she learned that her current conversion rate is 50%, which she thinks is low, especially since she accepts many of the kinds of insurance that people in her area have. The dashboard also indicates that the majority of her clients are finding her through her website. And she knows that the drop-off point is when the client is sent paperwork prior to their first appointment. After taking a quick look at her website and talking to other entrepreneurs in the same industry, she has a pretty good idea what the problem is.

Goal: The practice will convert enough of the right clients and increase its conversion rate from 50% to 75% in the next 45 days.

Interventions:

1. Heather will narrow her sales funnel by creating qualifiers on her website within the next seven days. She will clarify her message for her ideal client so that non-ideal clients will be less likely to enter the funnel and her conversion rate will be higher.

2. Heather will modify her call script to include a different strategy for her client care coordinator to use while on the phone with new leads.

3. Heather will manage potential clients' expectations on her website by clearly outlining the process in three steps. Since the supplemental data supported the assumption that clients were overwhelmed and therefore opted out of the funnel, she wants to prepare them for the client journey ahead of time.

When we look into Heather's treatment plan for her practice, we start to see that once the diagnosis was correctly outlined, the treatment interventions were fairly standard.

1. When Heather narrows her sales funnel, she will instantly improve conversion rates. Adding in qualifiers to deter clients that are inappropriate for Heather's practice will save her time and make her more money.

2. The script that Heather currently uses only generates a 50% conversion rate. Altering the script to show a sense of urgency, confidence in the clinicians, and her practice's authority in the industry has a high likelihood of increasing the conversion rate to meet the goal.

3. It's rare to find a highly converting website these days that does not utilize a three-step strategy. This is how you manage a client's expectations and pass along a sense of security in the process. People like to know what lies ahead, and this is the best way to do that!

As you design interventions to address the diagnoses in your practice, remember to utilize strategies that have the greatest likelihood of meeting the goal. It's important to also choose those interventions based on your practice's strengths. Work smarter, not harder, remember? Also, remember the client journey and the points along the way where they might opt out or get slowed down. You want to avoid this at all costs and be intentional in your planning.

Think about Amazon and how easy their buying experience is. It was easy all along, but now they have the "Buy it Now" button. Who can resist that? If you're on the fence here, unsure you're on board with my teaching point about simplifying the process, just give my FedEx driver a call. He'll tell you how well designed the "Buy it Now" button is.

In his book *Friction*, Roger Dooley tells the story of how Amazon proved itself as an industry genius because of its addition of that button.[19] Forget the cart, you can skip the entire checkout process and buy what you want with the click of one button. Amazon took all the friction out of the customer process and it is serving them well—they generated 280.5 billion dollars in 2019.[20]

Like Ernestina and Heather, the most important things for you to do are to get the diagnosis right, determine your goal, and think of the interventions as *how* you're going to get there. Don't worry, the interventions don't have to be perfect. There's no standardized procedure for where to start, and without speaking to you directly, there's no way I could pick an intervention for you. Just as you do when treating a patient, you will pick the interventions that you believe are most likely to work. Heck, some of them may not work, but some of them definitely will. You will never know until you try.

---

[19] Roger Dooley, *Friction: The Untapped Force That Can Be Your Most Powerful Advantage* (New York, NY: McGraw Hill, 2019).
[20] https://www.statista.com/topics/846/amazon/

ALIGN INTERVENTIONS WITH GOALS

Every action you take should be moving you toward meeting your goal. When you align your interventions, remember that if you make it easy for your clients to get what they need, they will. Think about what your clients like, dislike, or even despise. Do they have an aversion to talking on the phone? Are they busy professionals looking for something automated and simple? Do they not have time for the back and forth of emails and texts?

A perfect example of this is my hair salon. I know it's random, and I get some sideways looks when I bring it up, but I do own a hair salon. I'm not a stylist, an esthetician, or a lash lady. I'm an entrepreneur. I talk about the importance of ease in scheduling all the time to the beauty professionals who rent booths from me. Sometimes they listen, and sometimes they don't. But the ones who do have a lot more appointments booked.

Several years ago, before I owned a salon, I found a hair gal that I absolutely loved up in New Albany, Indiana. She is so amazing that, after my first appointment, I never considered going anywhere else. Plus, she has an easy system for meeting my scheduling needs. I own four businesses, and I have three kids and a husband who sometimes feels like my fourth child. I don't have time to get lost in a text novel about my next cut and color when it's time to schedule an appointment. Like Diana Jean at Mane Alley, you can be smart about considering your clients' journey. It works for her; she stays booked months in advance. Diana's salon is boutique-style and super niched, so her goal is to keep her schedules full and her clients showing up. One no-show would make a negative impact on her revenue. Since this is her goal, all of her interventions (scheduling features, fees, etc.) support it.

Another example of aligning interventions with goals comes from Jessica Tappana of Simplified SEO Consulting. Aside from the fact that she is an amazing human being, I love how Jessica makes SEO feel less scary for therapists trying to be found on Google. I met Jessica in 2017 while we waited at the Cherry Hill airport in Traverse City, Michigan, for a ride. We were both there to work on our mental health practices while staying at a boarding school repurposed as a place for people to slow down and get their creativity flowing. At the time, Jessica had the big idea of building a business around the one thing she had been so successful with: ranking number one on Google. She has a fee-for-service, trauma-focused practice in Missouri, where her clinicians carry full caseloads because of the SEO optimization she did on her website. Jessica mastered this so well in her own practice that she built a new business around it. She now helps practice owners move to the top of their rankings with genuine, honest, and strategic work. There are no smoke and mirrors with Jessica and her team, and to me, that's why she meets her goals.

My virtual assistant company is another example of designing interventions that align with goals. In this case, it is to help our clients achieve their goal of social media engagement. In 2018, I added a virtual assistant division to my consulting company out of pure necessity. I had a handful of clients who desperately needed social media content with purpose—content that would quickly inspire, problem-solve for, or provide information to the clients they served in their practices. We spent months analyzing the types of posts people engaged with and conducting countless interviews to find out why certain posts had lots of shares and engagements while other, equally attractive posts did not. What we discovered was that people engaged or shared when a post triggered an emotional response for them.

We're mental health professionals, and we almost totally missed the feelings part. We had to create content that elicited an emotional response from people so they would hit the share button even before they realized what they were doing. You know what I mean, scrolling the news feed at a red light when you're supposed to be watching for it to turn green? You're not taking into consideration who posted the content or why. You like it and you share it. Are you creating those types of captivating posts? The ones that make people want to follow you so they don't miss anything? If not, doing so could help you meet your goal of more client inquiries per day.

The point here is this: When you design interventions, they must be in alignment with the corresponding goal on your treatment plan. If your goal is to increase prospects to meet your sales need by using search engine optimization, every intervention you implement must serve the goal in order to achieve more client leads. The interventions would be focused on and specific to SEO, such as implementing the top ten keywords into the copy on your website. It could also mean you create five new subpages, each outlining a specialized service offered by your practice. Lastly, you could use social media to drive potential clients back to your website to get more traffic.

Do you see how each of these interventions are specifically aligned to the goal? When they are all in alignment, it's much easier to plan for progress and gauge the success of each specific action. It will also tell you what to tweak and what to enhance. Rather than having to watch multiple interventions with different corresponding goals, we can focus on the one diagnosis, the one goal, and all the interventions that serve it.

PICK THE INTERVENTION THAT WORKS

As a clinician, I loved the process of diagnosing because it reminded me of putting puzzles together with my granny when I was little. Once I was able to formulate the diagnosis, it was on to creating the treatment plan, including interventions that would yield the best results.

As medical professionals, we have found that once the diagnosis has been made, the interventions are often standard. It's the diagnosis that is the challenge—so many variables, so much information to sort through. Is the patient telling me the full story? What if what they're saying doesn't match the lab results? Once you're confident with the diagnosis, as hard as it may be, the interventions are there. You may have to think creatively, you may have to reach out for consultation, but it's unlikely that you will have to think of something so out-of-the-box that it's never been done before.

Do you see where I'm going with this? If the hardest part of the process is the diagnosis, thanks to the HHN, it has now become the easiest. We have done all the hard work for you so you can focus your efforts on creating a treatment plan for your business, because that's what it needs more than anything.

When I try to decide on the best intervention to include in my treatment plan, I like to start with free association. You've already identified your diagnosis, determined your baseline, and created your goal, so now you can start to generate all the possible ideas you could use as interventions to treat the problem. Once listed, you can begin to prioritize them based on their alignment to the goal, the time they would take to generate a ROI, and the ones that are most strongly associated with the diagnosis. When you are able to prioritize your interventions, you're then able to determine how much time, energy, and money you want to devote to each in order to achieve your goal as quickly as possible.

When you make these decisions, keep in mind that time does in fact equal money. If your goal is to increase leads and your interventions include using SEO, the specifics should be listed by order of effectiveness. If one intervention is to use social media to increase awareness of and share relevant blogs with your ideal client but you only have 150 followers, the likelihood that this intervention will be impactful is pretty low. You would need to first build a following so that when you do share a post or a blog, your ideal client actually sees it. You must consider the implications that the interventions you choose to implement will have for the goal. If the potential impact is low, I would suggest a new intervention, one that is more directly related to what you're trying to do. Perhaps an intervention like including more keywords people are searching for on your landing page, increasing the number of words, or using a blog to get backlinks and drive more traffic to your site would be more aligned with what you're trying to achieve.

Unfortunately, I can't tell you how to choose your intervention because there's too much variation from practice to practice. But what I can tell you is that, more often than not, it's not necessarily which intervention you choose, but how well you implement it and how much you follow through. People often say, "I tried that," and, "That didn't work," but when I start probing, I realize that they didn't commit to the intervention as much as they should. And people who make these comments never have a plan for progress—they never completely follow through. Do you choose the intervention that is best aligned with your own brand, values, and ethical considerations? It's going to look a little different for everyone, but as long as you commit to it and have a plan for progress, you will be on the right track. If in the end your intervention is not successful, move on to the next one with confidence.

APPLY INTERVENTIONS TO YOUR PRACTICE

Let's not overthink this. I've said this before, and I'll keep saying it until you can't get it out of your mind: Your business is like a patient; you just have to treat it that way. You will apply interventions to your practice in the very same way you apply them to a patient. It's also important to note that, when you apply interventions, you must also assign a designated person to oversee them. This goes back to the accountability piece that is so important. When people aren't given clear responsibility for a task and held accountable for the outcome, the likelihood that they will put forth enough effort for it to be successful is slim to none.

Apply your interventions with great intentionality. Be deliberate and strategic in your approach. This isn't the time to go all willy-nilly on me.

Remember, with the FTN system, we put all of our energy and focus on the one diagnosis that will make the most impact on your business. We're not addressing seven things at once; we're just focusing on one, which means all of our energy must go toward that. The interventions we employ must be clear, straightforward, and precise. If we decide to go with a social media campaign to drive leads to our practice, a great deal of thought must go into the topic of the campaign. Does it speak to my ideal client? Is there a possibility it could go viral? Is my call to action (CTA) strong? These are just a few of the many questions you could ask yourself when determining whether or not your intervention is a good one.

You want to ensure that before you apply any interventions to your practice's diagnosis, you have a way to track the results. If you're using social media, this might already be done for you under the Insights tab. Here, you can see your reach, engagements, likes, comments, shares, and an overall snapshot of how well people respond to your posts. Through Insight evaluation, your audience will actually tell you what they like and what they don't. From there, you can use the data to make modifications that further enhance the effectiveness of your intervention.

If your interventions are centered around a community-based marketing approach, you will need a different type of tracking system to measure the effectiveness of your actions. Many practice owners like to use dashboards in conjunction with their intake process. For example, when my practice delivers goodie bags to referral sources, they document the places they take the bags, whom they speak with, and the date. Using their referral tracking system, they can then match up the new leads that come in with the places the new leads have visited to determine if any new clients are a direct result of the marketing efforts. If you're going to spend money on it, you'd better track it.

Regardless of your approach, you must track the results of your interventions. Not only will this help you make decisions about meeting your goal, it will also help you get to know your ideal client in way that will allow you to better target your future marketing efforts. The best predictor of future behavior is past behavior. So why not apply this same idea to the way we conduct business? If, within the family practice space, you have found time after time that you get the greatest ROI when you publish an ad in the local *Family Wellness* magazine, then that makes determining interventions for future SALES diagnoses easy. Always do what works.

COMMON FIXES

Here is a list of commonly used interventions for each diagnosis in each of the five foundational levels. As a reminder, I just want to say that there's no right or wrong way to apply an intervention. I can't tell you which intervention to use because I don't know the details of your business. You'll treat your business in the same way you treat your patients—with interventions. As long as you apply an intervention to the right diagnosis, you're on the right track. It may not work, and in that case, you will have to choose another one. You may have to try five or six before you begin to see progress, but don't get down on yourself, frustrated, or throw in the towel if it doesn't work the first time. I'm not trying to confine you to an intervention box. I want you to push yourself, be creative, and be different. But in the event the most logical choice is the simplest one, here are several for you to choose from.

Potential Interventions for Identified Diagnoses

Do you remember when I said, at the beginning of the book, that there would be times when you'd want to slow your reading pace? This is one of them. This is also a great place to flag with a sticky note for easy reference later on. If you're anything like me, you might prefer to read through a book in its entirety first, then go back and spend more time with the sections that you need more time to process.

SALES *Interventions*

1. **Lifestyle Congruence Diagnosis**
   - Utilize a bookkeeper, accountant or CPA to help you determine if your productivity goals match your financial needs.
   - Evaluate your current productivity to establish a baseline.
   - Determine what's really necessary to live the lifestyle you desire.
   - Examine your monthly expenses. What is unnecessary and not moving your business toward its goal of profitability?
   - Determine the deficit—the gap between what you need and what you have.

2. **Prospect Attraction Diagnosis**
   - Can you create a social media campaign that has the potential to go viral? Use what's going on in your city as leverage to reach more people.
   - Use hashtags that potential prospects or providers may be searching for.
   - Take a strong stance in your social media game. When people know where you stand, they're more likely to follow you. Create a campaign for the purpose of taking a stand and watch your Insights daily to see what your audience responds to most.
   - Implement a text-to-talk campaign. You know, like "Text CARE2020 to 818181 to _____." (Example only.) This removes any barriers related to ease and accessibility so your clients can express interest at the exact moment when they need help.
   - Utilize local billboards to inspire hope and catch the attention of people in your community.

- Develop relationships with other community partners and refer to each other when possible.
- Make screening potential referrals easy for your community partners. Give them a quick checklist or assessment they could have their patients complete during the intake process. If patients meet a predetermined criterion, the community partner can then refer them to you.

Provider Attraction Diagnosis

- Build a reputation for behaving ethically and putting patients first by providing workshops that teach core skills for professionals in your area. All professional organizations require continuing education (CE), and this is one way that you could both offer CE credits and get in front of providers that might apply for a position with your company.
- Find something unique to become known for, whether it be a particular method of treatment, an outstanding luxury experience, or a zero-friction experience. Recognize who you are and embrace it.
- Stand out. Employ local artists to paint murals on your building, if it's one that you own. Support local charities that are looking for another business to get behind their efforts for change.
- Create a culture where your team is excited to come to work and wants all of their friends to come work with them.
- Offer recruitment bonuses for current staff to increase the chances that they will follow through on enticing former colleagues to your practice.
- Implement sign-on bonuses that are paid out over the course of an employee's first year.

- Offer to assist new hires in paying for an area of specialization or certification that would help round out your practice's clinical offerings.
- Invest in your providers professionally. Help them grow into stronger professionals with mentorship and encouragement.
- Create a virtual job fair and circulate it to all the local chambers of commerce, hiring companies, local universities, adult education centers, and anywhere else that would be likely to share it.

3. **Client Conversion Diagnosis**
   - Create your ideal client avatar and market specifically to them.
   - Be clear on the kinds of insurance you accept on your website and in any other type of marketing strategy.
   - Be specific about what you offer patients, so you spend less time turning away "unqualified" clients (i.e., clients who do not need your services). Tweak your system and train your staff to reflect these changes.
   - Smooth out the bumps in your intake process. Create a streamlined process in which each next step is as easy as possible and will not deter qualified clients.
   - Have scripts available that address each objection a client could have so you are prepared and confident in your answer.
   - Perhaps you understand the importance, but you don't have the manpower to oversee an intake department and it makes more sense to outsource it to a virtual assistant company like my friend Uriah's, The Productive Therapist.

4. **Delivering on Commitments Diagnosis**
   - Create standard operating procedures to ensure consistent care throughout the company.
   - Schedule weekly meetings with your team to check in on their adherence to delivering on commitments.
   - Add this section as a part of their employee performance evaluation.
   - Perform clinical quality assurance checks for every provider on your team.
   - Educate your team about what this concept really means. They can't adhere to something they don't understand.
   - Make sure that this is included in your company's overall mission statement to ensure that your employees are clear on what this really means as well as what it looks like for clients.

5. **Collecting on Commitments Diagnosis**
   - Conduct patient surveys to see if patients continue to work on their treatment plans (take medication, perform interventions, etc.) after they leave your office.
   - Put thorough policies in place to prevent no-shows or late cancelations.
   - Train your reception staff to reschedule appointments instead of canceling.
   - Put systems in place to track payments from insurance companies to ensure timely filing and reception of payments.

PROFIT *Interventions*

1. **Debt Eradication Diagnosis**
   - Put a plan in place to eliminate as much debt as possible by cutting unnecessary expenses.
   - Create a budget to ensure that your company runs on the revenue it generates.
   - Review all current expenses and find ways to cut costs within the organization. Take the savings and put it toward the elimination of debt so you can reduce it at a much faster pace.
   - Set up a plan to pay more than the minimum payment for all high interest-bearing accounts.
   - Seek out ways to consolidate debt if possible.
   - Look into refinancing options that will reduce the overall cost of the item or service you're purchasing.
   - Transfer high outstanding balances to a 0% APR credit card until you can leverage the debt in other ways to increase profit.
   - Utilize a monthly budget to restrict yourself from spending money on unnecessary expenses that will not increase your revenue or add to your profit margins.

2. **Margin Health Diagnosis**
   - Figure out how profitable each of your offerings is. How many times do you have to see a client before you turn a profit? Which services bring in the most revenue?
   - Find ways to maximize services that produce the most revenue and optimize the services that don't produce revenue, or as much revenue, immediately.
   - Consider raising rates to increase revenue.

- Avoid discounting or marking down the price of your service or offering unless there is a strategic way to leverage the loss for increased volume.

- Elevate your brand and increase the perceived value of the services you have to offer.

- Request rate increases from all the insurance companies and employee assistance programs (EAPs) with whom you currently work.

- Streamline your operations in order to reduce expenses and improve margin health.

- Consider other services, products, or offerings that you can add to your existing services.

- Identify and eliminate waste within the practice. What are you currently spending money on that is no longer needed? Could you go paperless?

- Explore the untapped potential of your employees. Can they do something to help increase profitability based on their skill set? Do they have a friend or family member with access to lower-cost products or services?

- Look at retention rates. The lower your acquisition costs, because your clients are repeatedly coming back to you, the greater your profit margins will be.

- Cut out the low payers. Don't waste your time and resources working just as hard to collect pennies on the dollar when you can cut out those payers/clients and focus your energy on the ones with higher margins.

3. **Appointment Frequency Diagnosis**
   - Track retention rates to see how often your patients return to your practice. Put a plan in place to have standing

appointments for all patients and providers within the organization.

- Use scheduling strategies, such as scheduling from noon backwards. Start at a noon appointment slot and continue to try and schedule backwards until you get to the earliest spot in the morning.

- Use appointment confirmations to secure appointments and provide your practice with the opportunity to replace a scheduled patient if they can no longer make the appointment. Many practices prefer to use text and email reminders. Some still like to use phone reminders so that they can also assess the patient's level of satisfaction, collect balances, and address any issues that may arise.

- Implement a patient-led appointment scheduling feature so patients can make their own appointments while cutting down on staff time used for scheduling.

- Consider offering more services that would benefit your ideal client.

- Create a system to schedule recurring, regular appointments whenever possible.

- Use patient recare and recall; in other words, reconnect with previous patients who have not been seen recently. This can be achieved through a spreadsheet system, with an email marketing campaign, or even with a simple survey.

4. **Profitable Leverage Diagnosis**

- To maximize leverage and make a gain, you need to make more money than you borrow plus the interest on the debt. Acquiring financial leverage isn't the goal. If you want to maximize profits with financial leverage, the key is to only borrow money that you believe can lead to increases in earnings beyond the full cost of the loan.

- Figure up the ROI on borrowed money after 30 days, 90 days, and 120 days.
- Set boundaries for yourself to ensure that any new debt will generate predictable, increased profit.
- Put a plan in place to quickly pay off new debt.

5. **Cash Reserves Diagnosis**
- Determine your operating expenses for six months. That is your cash reserves goal.
- Raise your rates to increase revenue. Put the difference of the increase toward your cash reserves goal.
- Rent out unused office space to professionals who complement the services you already offer.
- Temporarily redirect cash flow from one area of the business to your cash reserves.
- Find ways to tighten the budget. What can you temporarily live without or put off purchasing until after the cash reserves are secure?
- Negotiate rates with your insurance companies, landlords, utility companies, etc., to find extra funds to put into your reserves.
- To prevent unnecessary withdrawals from this fund, move the cash reserves to another bank or add another signer on the account.

ORDER *Interventions*

1. Systemization Diagnosis

- Teach each staff member the goal of their role in the company and help them prioritize the tasks that help them accomplish the goal.

- Ask each employee to list their process for each task within their role. Review the steps in the process and help them determine what is unnecessary or slowing down the process.

- To increase efficiency and improve margin health, streamline processes by reducing as many steps as possible.

- Automate steps in your processes to remove human involvement. This further increases your profit margins and reduces the likelihood of error.

- Delegate tasks that can be done by others so you can focus your time on things that others cannot do.

- Eliminate any tasks that are unnecessary and do not contribute to your goal of profitability.

- Empower staff members to find more efficient ways to complete tasks without compromising their goal or patient care.

- Occasionally observe systems to catch bottlenecks and congestion points.

2. Role Alignment Diagnosis

- Find out your employees' skills and strengths through the use of DiSC®, the Myers-Briggs Type Indicator, the CliftonStrengths assessment, the Riso-Hudson Enneagram Type Indicator (RHETI®), Sally Hogshead's Fascinate® test, or any other assessment designed to enhance productivity in the workplace.

- Use the results of these assessment measures to ensure that your staff are matched appropriately with their daily tasks.
- Whenever possible, align their roles with tasks they enjoy and are successful at.
- Reassign tasks that are clearly not in an employee's wheelhouse whenever possible.
- Implement a quarterly one-on-one meeting with each of your team members to review their productivity, effectiveness, and commitment to their current position.
- Promote people based on their skill set and the ROI they bring to the company.
- Encourage employees. Remind them of the company's *why,* and how they can contribute to it.
- Help employees express their future plans within the company and delineate the necessary action steps that will help them get there.
- Coach each employee based on whether they are driven by a need for achievement, affiliation, or power.
- Employ a strategy for sustaining momentum and success: include daily meetings, quick wins, team-building activities, annual retreats, unexpected incentives, public praise, etc.

3. **Outcome Delegation Diagnosis**
   - Empower your team to identify and solve problems within their own departments.
   - Clearly articulate the desired outcomes you have for each task or project within the company.
   - Remove yourself from the process and allow responsibility for the outcome to rest with your team.

- Teach your team to give, receive, and solicit healthy feedback to and from one another throughout the process.
- Delegate to the lowest level of the organizational development.
- Make sure to match the amount of responsibility with the amount of authority when assigning a task.
- Look at who is most motivated to successfully complete the task and assign it to them.
- Use the four-step method for delegation:
  1. Assess: Who is most motivated to complete this task, and who has the ability to do the task?
  2. Set Expectations: What do they need to do, and what does successful completion of this task look like?
  3. Provide Support: What authority does this person need to have to complete this task, how will you monitor progress and communicate throughout, and what will praise look like when this person successfully completes the task?
  4. Follow up: Does the employee clearly understand the expectations?

4. **Linchpin Redundancy Diagnosis**
   - Consider what information your employees have that you don't (passwords, keys, documents, etc.).
   - Create a plan to centralize and share these resources so that everyone who needs access can acquire access.
   - Create clear, concise, and usable standard operating procedures (SOPs).
   - Have employees switch roles in a controlled environment for a certain amount of time to test the clarity of the SOPs.

Take any questions generated during the exercise and use them to revise the SOPs. Keep the SOPs on file and frequently updated so they can be used if needed.

- Train at least one "backup" for every key role in the company.

5. **Problem-Solving Solutions Diagnosis**

- Implement the PASS Method™, which can be found in FTN QuickStart, or another problem-solving process.
- Require your team to track problems versus solutions and discuss the impact.
- Facilitate brainstorming sessions to help your team generate strategies to elicit change.
- Praise employees for offering solutions to problems independently.

The interventions you include in your practice's treatment plan will either move you forward, toward your goal, or hamper your progress. There are only two options. We have to understand that when we implement this new system, we will not be *doing* constantly. We will not pride ourselves on the eighty-two Post-It Notes plastered all over our office. We will put all of our focus and energy toward the one diagnosis that, once treated, will help us level up our practice.

It is now that I would encourage you to get support. Although it may feel like you run your business as a lone wolf most of the time, the truth is, you don't have to. You can join a number of small group coaching opportunities, masterminds, and accountability groups. You can become a partner in a membership community I designed specifically for healthcare entrepreneurs just like you.

I used to feel like I was running my practice in a bubble. I didn't know what others were doing and didn't even know how to find out. Once I built Mindsight Partners[21] and people just like you started to join, I began to see such an amazing transformation. Practice owners became more focused, they developed a stronger understanding of where they were going, and they no longer let fear stop them from improving. I love Mindsight Partners and everything it stands for. And if an online community is not right for you, go out there and find people in your area who are all working toward the same goal and do this thing together. When we are able to narrow the scope, and be deliberate in our treatment interventions, we all thrive.

There will be times when you are tempted back into that old mentality of *doing,* where you run your business as though you have all the time in the world, but all you're able to get out of it is exhaustion. It's okay; we all revert back to old habits when we're trying to form new ones. Stay strong and know that being focused and deliberate will take you where you have been trying to go.

---

[21] https://www.mindsightpartners.com

Chapter Eight

Plan for Progress

ONE MANTRA IN THE HEALTHCARE FIELD IS: "IF IT'S NOT written down, it didn't happen." While most certainly true, I'll take it one step further. *If it's not written down, it's not going to happen.* If you spent the time to read this book, if you spent the time solving problem after problem, hoping that at least one of them will actually make an impact, then please spend an additional five minutes and write down the plan so you can get maximum results.

When people are left to their own devices, they will always take the easiest route. Just because your office manager knows she has a Collecting on Commitments diagnosis, since patients are not paying on time, it doesn't mean she will address the problem in a manner you'll be happy about. Just because she has the list of interventions and knows exactly what to do, it doesn't mean she'll do them with the frequency and intensity that you would like. Just because she knows that revenue has dropped, it doesn't mean that she will know to make it top priority without accountability from you and the plan.

While it may feel like an afterthought, the plan for progress is one of the most important components of the treatment for your business's diagnosis. The plan is where most people fail and the place where most people give up. The plan is where accountability comes into play. This is where we discuss the intensity and frequency of the intervention, who's responsible for what, and when it will be reevaluated. Just like a patient, a business owner and their team are much more likely to follow through with a task if there is a measurement of accountability.

Think about the plan for progress for your business in the same way you think about your patients. You put forth all of your expertise, your knowledge, and your experience to create goals and interventions because they're sick and they need you. You are the one they turn to and, in many cases, their last resort.

Take yourself back to a time when you felt disappointment in a patient who *could* (in every sense of the word) have had a positive prognosis *if* they followed their plan.

But they didn't.

You see them a month later for a follow-up visit and they didn't do one thing you laid out for them, despite the fact that you spent half an hour educating them about the worst-case scenario, what could happen if they don't put their health and wellness first. Here they are, and they haven't done the first thing. How frustrating is that? This is why the plan is so important. Your business needs a plan for progress. You need accountability to make that vital change to take it to the next level.

THE PLAN PROVIDES CONFIDENCE

She can sense the uncertainty that her night shift brings, as it does each time she takes the elevator to the second floor. She smells the pungent aroma of disinfectant and the odor of fear as she enters the neonatal unit of her local hospital. She whispers a prayer right before she pushes the button that opens the heavy double doors. She reminds herself of her *why* as she suits up for the night.

It's almost time for her shift to start and the first sound she hears is a baby's cry. She can almost identify each baby by the unique pitch of their voice and the pattern of their whimpers. Neonatal nurse Jennifer says that her years and experience in the field give her the confidence to work with babies who don't yet have a voice. "Feeling vulnerable in moments of fear and facing the unknown is what propels me to keep learning," she said when asked about how it helps her to have a plan. "I know that in each situation, with each new patient, and in each new case, there's an opportunity to learn."

Jennifer has treated babies for the majority of her career and wouldn't have it any other way. She creates a plan for every patient, not just because it's best practice and policy, but because that's what makes her feel better about the goal she's working toward. If a certain treatment intervention is unsuccessful, she makes modifications to the plan in order to achieve a better outcome. Just as you will when you treat your business, Jennifer finds confidence in having a plan.

Imagine that you struggle to retain employees. There's more turnover than you think is normal and you want to do something about it. This is an unmet Core Need in the foundational level of **SALES**, so it becomes your diagnosis. You love your practice, and you don't understand why people keep leaving. You chalk it up to the season of change—everyone needs to move on—but in the back of your mind. you wonder if you're just fooling yourself. People have left to make more money in the past, but there's just nothing in the margins to pay people more. In fact, there are times when you can barely make payroll, times when you sacrifice your own paycheck so your staff can have theirs. But they don't know that.

Your business isn't necessarily suffering, from a profitability standpoint, because you replace people quickly and seem to recover okay. But they are leaving, and you don't want them to. Although the dashboard doesn't indicate a problem, it can't show how much energy is used to recover from each letter of resignation. It doesn't show how much time it takes to inventory the tasks the person was once responsible for, create the new position, screen all the applicants, interview the most qualified ones, and onboard the one you think is most capable of meeting the needs of the practice. The dashboard doesn't show how much emotional turmoil this causes you and your administrative staff, or the self-doubt, the questioning: "Is my practice not good enough? Do I not pay enough? Do I *not* show people that I value them?" It's hard to say exactly how much this impacts you, but you know it's a lot. Time and time again, when someone leaves, you can't help but feel defeated.

Since this has happened many times before, you are now equipped with a plan. And although it still stings a bit each time you receive a letter of res-ignation, the swelling doesn't last as long because you have a plan. You have a plan to prevent employee turnover, and you also have a plan to handle it when it does happen. These plans will give you confidence and the ability to look at the situation objectively, as you would a patient. It takes the emotion out of it; after all, we can't run our businesses on feelings.

LET'S "DRAW IT OUT"

I come from a family of doers. We're not afraid to roll up our sleeves, put on our boots, and get to work. We don't work till we're hungry or tired, we work till the job is done. My dad, whom I like to call "the Old Man," is seventy years old, but you wouldn't know it. I have to keep an eye on him because if he sets out on a project, you won't see him again until it's finished. He'd kill me if he knew I was telling this story, but I've never seen him read a book, so I'll take my chances.

When I was a kid, there was an old maple tree that separated the space between my dad's trailer and my grandparents' house. I remember the coarseness of its trunk and how it reminded me of my poppy's skin. The trunk's rough, uneven surface peeled and flaked beneath my little bare feet as I scrambled up to the top. It popped and cracked as I climbed, making me feel as alive as any eleven-year-old could feel. Sometimes, as I made my ascent, my toes stuck to the sap that dripped from my favorite nooks and crannies in the branches.

Every now and then there was a battle to fight with black ants, but nevertheless, I claimed it. It was my tree. It stood dead center on the side of the property closest to the road, looking over the garden Poppy tilled with his own two hands. I remember as if it was yesterday that the pumpkins were planted in the row closest to his house, and the bodacious corn was planted in the row closest to my dad's. In between, you would find the tomatoes, potatoes, green beans, and watermelons, enough variety to keep our dinner plates colorful and our bellies full. At one point, Poppy decided to grow peanuts in the back of the garden, furthest away from my tree, which made for some of the most amazing peanut brittle and some fantastic memories.

From the treetop, I could see everything. After all, I had to keep an eye on the place. As a kid, spying was my favorite thing to do. I remember climbing up to the highest branch early in the morning to set my sights on anything that looked the least bit interesting. Most mornings, Poppy and the Old Man would meet halfway between their two houses to "draw out" the day. Most of the time, they didn't even notice me sitting twenty feet above them, eavesdropping.

"This corn's coming in nice, isn't it?" Poppy would say.

"Hmph," I'd hear come from Dad's direction. "Those beans are about dead," he'd mutter.

You see, neither of them were the friendliest with each other. If one said something was green, the other would swear it was brown, and so on and so forth. Which is why their morning meetings were so funny to me. They'd both show up after coffee to bicker a little before Poppy gave the go-ahead, and then they'd start on a project.

One morning, there was more of a nip in the air than usual. I should have known something was about to go down. There I was, up in my tree, while the two grown men stood below me and argued about the most efficient way to clean the gutters.

"Go over there in the corner of the garage and grab the gutter bucket!" Poppy ordered.

"Gutter bucket? Welp. Hmph! What the hell is that?" the Old Man asked.

"Ronnie Mitchell, you know what a gutter bucket is. It's the bucket you're going to carry when you climb up the ladder and clean out my gutters."

"Like hell. That's what a leaf blower is for."

"I don't trust that electric garbage. You're going to do it the old-fashioned way. Now go get the bucket," Poppy demanded.

Dad didn't respond because you didn't argue with Poppy. No one did. He was always right, always perfect. They both stormed off in different directions, most likely cursing each other under their breath the entire time. The Old Man thought Poppy was a time-waster, and Poppy thought the Old Man was a half-asser. A couple of minutes later, I saw my dad walking toward the ladder Poppy had propped up against the house, carrying a white five-gallon bucket. They were too far away for me to hear, so I made my way down the tree and on to my next adventure. I'd had my daily dose of excitement, and I see in retrospect that I'd also gained a better understanding of why I like a good plan.

Just like Poppy and the Old Man used to meet under my tree to "draw out" the day, I wake up each morning and "draw out the day" in my Moleskine notebook. There was no such thing as half-assin' when my grandpa was around; he expected perfection, from himself and from everyone around him. You were going to do it right, or you weren't going to do it at all. I'd venture to guess that all of us have a little Poppy in us, and maybe a little of the Old Man too. There's that part of us that likes a good plan and needs to "draw it out" to perfection before making any important decisions, and another part of us that craves efficiency and just wants to plow right through knowing that the work may not be perfect—there may still be a leaf in the gutter—but at least it's done.

I find myself somewhere in the middle, like the maple tree overlooking the garden. There needs to be a balance of both, and that's why my dad and grandpa's system worked so well. They balanced each other's work styles and served as each other's accountability partners. My dad needed more of a plan and to pay a little more attention to the details, and Poppy sometimes needed to plow on through so the job could get done. In his rigidity, Poppy often forgot that not everything had to be perfect. Sometimes he needed a reminder that it was about the progress, not perfection. I can thank my Old Man for teaching both of us that lesson.

The lesson I want to teach you is this: It's always helpful to have a plan for navigating your entrepreneurial journey. Aiming for perfection can cause a rigidity that will restrict creativity, and you don't want that. You must realize that your plan is a guide; it's what keeps you on track, what keeps you focused on your goal. Always make time to "draw out the day," but rather than focusing on perfection, aim for progress instead.

PROGRESS, NOT PERFECTION

In my practice, I designate an employee to be the accountability police for three reasons.

1. I still tend to have a little more Poppy in me than I do Old Man. To combat this, I purposefully move from one project to another quickly, so I don't give myself time to get caught up in the details.
2. It requires a lot of mental energy to track all the tasks and the progress being made on each. My energy is better spent on other things.
3. I don't like holding others accountable.

You may need an accountability police officer too, especially if you can relate to any of the three reasons why I have one. Accountability is woven into your business's treatment plan; you make sure that you have someone who understands its importance and will follow through with the actions you include. There are three important components that you must make sure are included in your Plan for Progress. They are simple but critical.

1. **Frequency:** How often will you employ these interventions?
2. **Intensity:** To what extent will you employ these interventions?
3. **Accountability:** Who is responsible for each of these interventions?

ERNESTINA'S TREATMENT PLAN

Presenting Problem: Ernestina does not have enough new leads coming in to fill her clinicians' schedules.

Baseline: The call log shows that she's receiving approximately three calls per day and is scheduling two appointments per week for new clients. Her new clients have heard about her through a commonly used platform in her area. She pays a fee for the use of the platform, and the platform sends referrals to her.

Diagnosis: Prospect Attraction

Specific Goal: The practice will receive 10 new leads per day by narrowing the funnel.

Interventions:
1. Create an email marketing campaign using the emails of all the referral sources you have collected since your practice started.

- **Plan for Progress:** Ernestina's virtual assistant (VA) (accountability) will set up the marketing campaign in the next 5 business days (frequency) to include all the current referral sources and their exported email addresses. She will send out the first email campaign and check the analytics on day 30 (intensity) once the sequence is finished.

2. Put work into the SEO of your website with the help of a trusted business—like Jessica Tappana's Simplified SEO Consulting.

   - **Plan for Progress:** Ernestina (accountability) will reach out to Simplified SEO Consulting in the next 3 days (frequency) to set up a meeting about utilizing SEO services for her website. She will plan to have her website optimized within the next 30 days (intensity) and review the improvements with the team 30 days after completion.

3. Up your social media game by pumping out content that helps people quickly.

   - **Plan for Progress:** Ernestina will utilize her VA (accountability) for this single (frequency) task. The VA will create social media content for the upcoming month 30 days in advance (intensity). The goal of the social media campaign is to increase followers and drive traffic to the website that Ernestina is optimizing. The VA will review social media insights weekly in order to determine the type of content Ernestina's audience is responding to best, then increase production of that kind of content. She will measure the effectiveness of the strategy by exporting the insights to a shared dashboard for Ernestina to see.

4. Make the process for getting an appointment easy. Think about the client journey, asking yourself: How do most clients prefer to be scheduled? Accommodate them!

   • **Plan for Progress:** Since people are looking for convenience, Ernestina (accountability) will implement an EZ Texting campaign in the next 5 days (frequency) that allows potential clients to text a number like "CARE2020," entering them into her sales funnel. This text feature triggers her intake process, so there's no additional work to do; it's just a quick and easy starting point for clients. Since it is new and interesting, she decides to have her VA (accountability) incorporate it into the social media campaign and post weekly (intensity), with the goal of gaining traction toward more leads. Ernestina will meet with her VA monthly to review the statistics of the EZ Texting campaign.

5. Formulate an email marketing nurture campaign to send to the exported client emails from your Electronic Healthcare Records (EHR), giving clients a simple call to action so they can get back in easily.

   • **Plan for Progress:** While Ernestina's VA is creating the email marketing campaign for referral sources, Ernestina (accountability) will create a second campaign for clients. She will export client emails from her EHR system and import them into the marketing campaign. She will design a set of 5 emails (intensity) for the nurture campaign that will go out over the course of the next 8 weeks (frequency). She will include a call-to-action button in each email to make the client's journey easy. She will evaluate the effectiveness of the campaign after each email is sent and watch her referral dashboard to see if more referrals come in as a result of a particular email.

Do you remember Heather and her Client Conversion diagnosis? Here, we want to include the plan for progress to ensure that there is both accountability for and deliberate action toward meeting her goal of increasing client conversion from 50-75%.

HEATHER'S TREATMENT PLAN

Diagnosis: Client Conversion

Baseline: The practice is currently converting approximately 50% of all new leads.

Specific Goal: The practice will increase client conversion from 50% to 75% in the next 45 days in order to support its level of needed billable sessions.

Interventions:

1. Heather will narrow the funnel by creating qualifiers on her website within the next seven days. Heather will clarify her message for her ideal client so that non-ideal clients will be less likely to enter the funnel and her conversion rate will increase.

- **Plan for Progress:** Every seven days (frequency), Heather (accountability) will evaluate the quality of the website's leads based on her web hosting platform's statistics and information from her intake dashboard. Heather will gauge whether or not narrowing the funnel was successful and identify if there are any other modifications that need to be made. If so, she will implement the change immediately (intensity) and track for progress.

2. Heather will modify her call script to include a different strategy for her client care coordinator (CCC) to use.

   - **Plan for Progress:** The CCC (accountability) will begin using the new script within the next fourteen days (frequency) and note the change on the referral tracking dashboard daily (intensity). Heather and the CCC will review the effectiveness of the modified script weekly, making changes as needed. With the qualifiers already in place with intervention one, the new leads coming into the practice should be much more qualified than before. This will allow Heather and her CCC to get a much more accurate assessment of the effectiveness of the script.

3. Heather will manage potential clients' expectations on her website by clearly outlining the process in three steps.

   - **Plan for Progress:** Since the supplemental data supported the assumption that clients were overwhelmed and therefore opting out of the funnel, Heather wants to prepare them for the client journey ahead of time. Heather (accountability) will install this new, simple 3-step method on her website within the next 7 days (frequency) and review the referral dashboard at the end of her 45-day objective (intensity), after its implementation. She will look for client conversion statistics, specifically noting how many clients successfully complete the process.

Many people skip over the most important part. You must review the effectiveness of the results. You must believe yourself, and communicate to your team, that once an intervention is implemented, evaluating progress is key. Want to know if a particular intervention is working, and if not, why? This alone will help you make informed decisions in the future, when another Client Conversion diagnosis presents itself. Rather than starting from scratch, you just pull out a former treatment plan, find the intervention that was successful before, and do it again. Most importantly, remember: it's about progress, not perfection.

ALL FOR NOTHING

In his book *Looking for Alaska*, John Green says, "Everything that comes together falls apart. Everything. The chair I'm sitting on. It was built, and so it will fall apart. I'm gonna fall apart, probably before this chair. And you're gonna fall apart..."[22]

If you're not constantly pushing, challenging, and nurturing it, any system will tend toward chaos and collapse. This is where your plan comes into play. Holding people accountable keeps the chaos at bay. Whether your

---

[22] John Green, *Looking for Alaska* (New York, NY: Penguin Books, 2006).

team will admit it or not, they want structure. They want accountability, they want goals, and they want a process to follow.

When I was going through my undergraduate program in elementary education, my professors loved to tell us that our "future students" wanted rules and craved structure.

Yeah, right.

I was a young new teacher, just twenty-one years old. I was barely old enough to get into a bar, but I'd been entrusted with a large group of sixth-graders. The principal had plucked me from my student teaching experience early because she was in desperate need of a history teacher. She had only known me for a few short weeks, and had no idea whether or not I was prepared to be a middle school teacher.

I'm not prepared for this, I thought during the week that led up to my big first day.

I went to college to teach elementary school students. El-e-men-ta-ry, ELEMENTARY! Not to wrangle prepubescent boys running around like hormonal Tasmanian devils. Not to engage in backtalk battles and power struggles over whether or not it's a human right to go to the bathroom every three minutes.

I had always pictured a neatly organized, colorful classroom with sight words and lists of my favorite adjectives on the walls, crepe paper globes hanging from the ceiling, and a little lighted reading nook over in the corner where my second-graders could cuddle up on a beanbag with a teddy bear and their favorite *Berenstain Bears* book. I had imagined myself standing there before my class of eighteen eight-year-olds, all of them sitting nicely in their seats, all eyes and ears on me, ready to learn. When I asked them a question as I wrote on the dry-erase board, they would eagerly raise their little hands, so excited they would practically jump out of their chairs. They would be sweet; they would hug me, draw me pictures, and beg to walk beside me as we moved from one place in the building to another.

What I got instead were sixth-graders with facial hair and body odor that could stop you dead in your tracks. My first day on the job was absolutely terrifying. I woke up early, got to school early, and walked into my classroom alone. The walls were a dirty shade of white, and on the wall, instead of multicolored sight words, I saw used bubble gum and what looked to be the dried remains of vomit or a mishap with rice pudding. The only thing that looked familiar or the least bit comforting was a single flower, a white daisy, sitting in a smidgen of water in a Styrofoam cup on my desk. There was a note propped against the cup.

"Have a great first day. And GOOD LUCK. You're going to

need it. —The Teacher Next Door."

Oh gawd, is he trying to tell me something? Should I grab my purse and leave now? It's not too late, I still could run. As I panicked, in walked my first student. We made eye contact and I was paralyzed. I breathed in through my nose and out through my mouth and swallowed hard. The lump in my throat wouldn't go down.

I searched my brain as if it were a filing cabinet. I sorted through all the things I had learned in school, desperately looking for the right thing to say. I didn't know how to start, where to start, or what to do. And then I heard them.

They stampeded into the room like wildebeests, running, laughing, and jumping over desks. They looked at me like I was an alien. Heads cocked to the side and eyebrows furrowed. *Who is this kid?* I suspected they thought. From the back of the room, I heard someone yell, "Floppy!" followed by a shriek of pain. I didn't look because I was too scared to know. I turned around and one student stood inches from my face, just looking at me. No words, just staring. I felt like I was in a zoo, a literal zoo, and at that point I didn't know if I was one of the animals. I was definitely NOT equipped to be the zookeeper. Where was my tranquilizer gun?

I quickly weighed my options, the first one still being that I could run. I considered how loud I would have to yell before another teacher heard me. Would "Heads up, seven up!" work? Wait, no, these were middle schoolers, not kindergarteners! I didn't know what to do. For a few moments, I succumbed to their behavior. I stood there and stared right back at them. Not at anyone in particular, just the blur of the vomit-stained wall. I was trying to pull myself together.

Despite the fact that one student lay on top of a table and threw a squishy ball into the air, another student ate his boogers, and the one over to my left was giving every boy in the room a floppy, I could hear the screams of the students in The Teacher Next Door's room and they were just as loud. He had a zoo too, and his animals were just as wild as mine.

Maybe it wasn't really that bad. "Students crave structure, even when they act like they don't," I remember my professor, Dr. Bowen, telling us. Maybe he was right. That was all I knew, so that's what I gave them—and at that point, I didn't have much to lose. I created morning routines, homework submission routines, a process for asking questions and receiving feedback, and a system for using the restroom without disrupting the entire class.

My students started to come around, and with that little bit of structure and a whole lot of grace, my little Tasmanian devils became the ones to watch. They were complimented by visitors and encouraged by the administration, and they shocked my team of fellow teachers with their ability to conform to my plan. When they were given the structure to achieve order, they flourished. What started as an expectation ended with a group of twenty-one students actually learning. Even better than that, they had become a group of twenty-one students who knew that they had no cap. They began to see their own potential and realize that, despite their physical or intellectual limitations, they were capable.

You see, in my first group of students ever, half were identified as having special needs and the other half were just wild. But they were all rising because of order and thriving because of confidence—all because I had a plan for them.

Your employees, your team, and your business also need the structure of a plan in order to thrive. After all, that's all it took for my wildebeests to flourish. Once I was able to stand with confidence, outline the day, and communicate my expectations to my zoo, my little animals excelled and I finally became the zookeeper I needed to be. Actually, that's not true. At that point, my animals became students, and I went from being their zookeeper to their teacher, their leader who had a plan.

Your business can and will do the same as my classroom, as long as it has a plan. The plan is what ties everything together. It's the icing on the cake, the bow on a beautifully wrapped gift, the cherry on top of a sundae. The plan is where you proclaim your commitment to solving the identified problem (diagnosis), the interventions you will make, and the people you will put in place to resolve the issue. It's the thing that gives us hope that our efforts are not in vain, the thing that gives us confidence to move forward despite our hardships, and the thing that will level up our practice.

Conclusion

You Can
and You Will

LILLIE, WILLIE, AND ZILLIE WERE THEIR NAMES: A SET OF TRIP-
lets born back in the spring of 1921, in a little shack off the main road in
Fonthill, Kentucky. Nestled in a cove on the Cumberland River, nearly hid-
den by the bigleaf magnolia that happened to be in bloom already, the house
sat proudly. Some may have seen it as mere planks of lumber nailed up by
hand to support a small but mighty frame, but Lillie, Willie, and Zillie
didn't care. The strength of their family's foundation wasn't tied to how
many bedrooms their homeplace had or whether or not it had an indoor
toilet, which it didn't. It wasn't about the earth that peeked through the
cracks in the floorboards or the smell coming up from the dirt after a hard
rain. It was tied to what the family stood for and how they instilled purpose
in the bones of each and every one of their twelve children.

Lillie was the strong-willed one. Her frame too was small, but she was
ever so mighty. Her skin was tan from the Kentucky sun, and her dirty-
blonde curls hung above her often furrowed brow. She was resourceful, and
always made the most of what she had, which wasn't much. Her no-non-
sense personality and dry sense of humor helped her survive. She was logical enough to know that she could never do everything to keep her family
from being poor, but what she could do was important to her. It made her
who she was. It's what drove her to push through the pain when her hands
went from blistered to bleeding, and then to calloused, from working the
wheelbarrow sunup to sundown.

Her days working on the farm were long and grueling, but she never complained. She focused on that which was in her control, that which would help tend to the biggest need they faced as a family. She knew there was work to be done and the tobacco wasn't going to strip itself. She wasn't a lofty dreamer—she didn't believe in indulging in the temptations of the world—but she had an internal compass that never steered her in the wrong direction. She may have not had idealistic adventures planned for her future, but she always knew where she was going. And she never tried to do it all, because the work was never done. She stayed strong, took life day by day, and focused on what would make the most impact at any given time.

Lillie's childhood was spent working on the farm. Then, the day she turned fifteen, she traveled one state to the north, to Indiana, to work as a canning factory assembly worker for the season. It wasn't prestigious, but it helped pay the bills and that's what the family needed. She was used to this kind of work back at home, canning cucumbers, tomatoes, and green beans, doing all those things that most people don't anymore. It was her first real job and the start of her independence. Like many of her fifteen-year-old coworkers, Lillie tried to embrace her new life away from home and kept her eye on earning money to send back for the young'uns. She didn't think about what she would do when she returned home, or where she would live if she married that boy Daddy wanted her to; she knew that right then her family needed money, and she could help provide it.

Kids weren't kids very long back in the 1920s. They were expected to get jobs, get married, and start their own families. When Lillie returned from the Hoosier State, it wasn't long before she got married too. The years passed quickly, and before she knew it, she was twenty-eight years old and giving birth to her second daughter in the back of her grandfather's Ford Model A.

She was the first to wake every morning in order to get the house warm before the children started to stir. It took two fires to shake the chill off, one in each of their potbellied stoves. She'd entice them out of bed at sunrise with the smell of her famous country biscuits, always made entirely by hand with freshly churned butter. Sometimes, if the kids were good, she'd make chocolate gravy for them to dip their biscuits in. At this point in her life, Lillie wasn't focused on saving up for a bigger house, or sending her children out for higher education; it was all she could do keep food on the table, fire in the stove, and the tobacco tended.

Lillie and her husband, Pat, were what most would call old-fashioned. They were the doers of deeds that needed done. Nothing fancy or unnecessary ever entered their lives. He didn't like her to go out much because she was a housewife and belonged at home. Since she rarely left the homeplace, there was no good reason for her to have more than two dresses. She listened to her husband because that's what wives were expected to do. She cared for the house, tended the garden, taught her children right from wrong, and became the noble pillar of the family.

One day, Lillie got a ride to town. She stopped in at Gadberry's Grocery in Eli to grab some necessities, as she did ever so often. She kept her head down and stayed to herself while carefully marking the items off her list. She didn't want to draw any attention her way, because that's not kind of person she was. While there, she caught a wild hair and decided to pick up a couple bags of flour instead of just the one. As she approached the register, she told the man behind it, Floyd Gadberry, to charge it to her account. This is what she did every time she shopped at the store, because she wouldn't have the money to pay until her tobacco check came in. Floyd didn't mind because he knew Lillie was good for it.

During the Great Depression, flour sacks were made of cotton, and sometimes the material was quite lovely. Lillie was used to being resourceful and had often used these sacks to sew her children's clothes, ever since they were babies. When Pat died in 1973, Lillie was fifty-two years old. She'd only ever known one life and that was the one with him in it. Pat was a good man, but a controlling one. She had never been allowed to go to church because he wasn't a believer. She had never driven a car because she never needed to, and remember, he only ever saw the need for her to have two dresses. With Pat gone, Lillie had no choice but to set aside her fears of the unknown and get out into the world. With no one to depend on but herself, she needed to decide how she was going to spend her time.

I can't imagine what Lillie felt at this point in her life. Did she feel lost? We are not sure, but one thing is certain: It didn't take long for the fabric from the flour sacks to become the basis for Lillie's new direction in life— her third, fourth, and before anyone knew it, a closet full of dresses. These dresses were the first of Lillie's possessions that weren't justified by need. They were her way of finding herself in a world that felt like it never even belonged to her. It was her way of saying, "Look at me, I can take care of myself, by myself."

Lillie had no control over it, but she was born with a disadvantage. She was poor, she wasn't formally educated, and she was often looked over. She married into a world of rules, restrictions, and rigidity. She went from one unfortunate situation to another, but one thing of hers never wavered. She always relied on her compass to point her in the direction she needed to go, keeping in mind what mattered most. She always used what she had to get what she didn't. She always had a plan. This allowed her to live her life the way she wanted: with her head held high, in a cotton dress made from her own two hands, and her feet always pointed toward her true north.

She wasn't an entrepreneur in the way that we think of one. She was a homemaker who figured out how to monetize her talent of sewing.

"Lillie, you know the Russell County Fair is coming up, are you thinking about entering a quilt for the auction?" the local pastor would ask as he called to check in.

"I reckon I could, the good Lord willin'," she'd say back, just as serious as all get-out.

It just so happened, that year her quilt got so much attention that she was featured in a favorite Kentucky magazine, *Taste of Home.* She would never have considered herself a local celebrity, but her talent for quilting won her *many* a blue ribbon at the Russell County Fair. She was an artist; her attention to detail was out of this world. Perfect and consistent stitching made it hard to tell that her quilts weren't made with a sewing machine, and she took pride in that. Before she knew it, she had orders coming in, enough to fill up an entire year with work. She was truly a gem; a gift, with an unrelenting talent that she never even knew she had. Fortunately for her, others did, and she was paid well for her gifts. At this point in her life, she had one concern, and that was making enough money to care for herself, her adult children, and her new home with an indoor toilet.

She figured out how to provide for six children and ten grandchildren just as well as anybody, even if that somebody had much more money. Even into their adulthood, her children could rely on their mom to help them if they found themselves in a bind. She provided the sense of stability in the family. And she was the one you always knew would buy you a pack of socks or underwear for Christmas, even when she was barely able to buy them for herself, and even when you were twenty-five years old.

My grandma Lillie was a special lady. She was quiet, with an unassuming but powerful presence. When she spoke, people listened. She found comfort in having a plan, much like I do and much like Poppy did. She was not one to worry, or waste energy on the what-ifs, and neither am I (unless I'm on an airplane). She put every ounce of effort into what she believed would work and let her faith take care of the rest. I felt a special kind of connection with her, but I could never put my finger on what it was.

When the baby who was born in the back of the Ford eventually shared these stories of my grandma Lillie with me, I started to understand. Mom said my connection to Granny was because she was always intentional, so her life was full of purpose and meaning. Perhaps it was that she was an artist in her own right, and I could relate to that. I guess it could have been that she told people exactly what she thought, with no apologies, and that helped me understand her more. She was the most authentic human being, and that left an imprint on my heart. No moment was ever wasted, and she spent "nary a bit" of time doing anything that did not serve her heart's goal.

I didn't know it as a kid, but my granny Lillie's internal compass would one day become my own. It was more than just the memories of learning to crochet, or her hands teaching me to make peanut butter fudge the same way her granny had taught her. It was the part that was even more rare; the part you couldn't teach, and that you most certainly couldn't learn. It was the part that even I cannot explain. It was just there, inside of me, patiently waiting for me to step up and have the confidence to ask it where I should go in life.

When she passed, I was in my early twenties and proud to carry on her purpose. I hold her strong will and grit, her determination, and her internal sense of life's direction deep in my bones. This is what keeps me centered and what gives me the confidence to always follow *my* true north. This is what I hope to pass along to my children one day, so that, whether in business or in life, they never feel lost and never go a day without being intentional.

We do not have to do all the things, because there will never be a shortage of things. And when we try, we can lose our sense of direction. We have to do the one thing that will make the biggest impact at any given time. We just have to go back to the basics and do more of what we already know. We must work on our business with deliberate action, focusing on the vital need that will make the most impact in moving us closer toward our goal, our true north.

My granny focused on different things throughout her lifetime, but always gave attention to the most important thing at any given time. In the beginning, it was all about survival. For herself, her siblings, and then the young'uns of her own. When that was secure, we began to see her focus more on herself, who she was, the impact she would have, and the legacy she would leave behind. Like Granny Lillie, we have the opportunity to leave a legacy. We do that through satisfying our sales needs, being purposeful with our profit margins, and establishing efficiency and order to take some of the pressure off.

When you can look at your practice through this new FTN lens, you will always have clarity around your direction, your diagnosis, and your compass. When you can name it, you can treat it. When you can treat it, you can heal it. That's what we're doing here. We're healing our business, we're restoring our energy, we're taking back our time. We're saying, "Enough is enough, I want my freedom. You will no longer dictate my life, business. You will serve *me*, like I designed you to. And if you don't, I will diagnose you, and I will fix you. Whether you like it or not!"

With your compass in hand, you can be like Ernestina, who now finds joy in problem-solving instead of viewing problems as failures. You can be like Heather, who is down off the struggle bus for good because she knows she always has a roadmap. Maybe you will be like Cathy, who stopped trying to run her business like a therapist and started running it like the badass boss lady she truly is. You can be like Katie, who now has more than enough cash reserves to leverage her business in any way she sees fit. You can be like any of the hundreds of people who send me emails, DMs, and comments on social media about the transformation they have seen from using this system.

You see, treating your business like a patient puts *you* in the driver's seat. It brings you back to that sense of control and empowerment. When you drive the bus, you control the destination, and your destination is profitability, my friends. You are healthcare entrepreneurs because you want to help people. You want to see lives changed and you believe there is a better way. You want freedom to go on family vacations and create a work schedule that isn't a catalyst for burnout. Why? Because you deserve it. When you're driving your own bus, according to your own map, toward your own destination, it's liberating. Although the destination is the point, what you find along the way is what matters most.

And do you know what that is?

When you employ the FTN system I have taught you in this book, you will achieve success. You will spend less time trying to prioritize your to-do list, and more time deciding what you're going to do *next*. I am on a mission to help business owners *find* their entrepreneurial confidence, and this is how you're going to do it. Throughout your journey navigating diagnoses, goals, and interventions, you will find something that may have been sitting dormant inside of you all along. You will find the confidence to be bold, run your business like a boss, and ask yourself one question and never be afraid of the answer: "What's next?"

I have been blessed to help so many people systemize their businesses. In several of these scenarios, this has generated millions of dollars in increased revenue, and for that people always thank me. It is my greatest honor to help others achieve success, but the most impactful part is the way they sit up a little straighter, speak a little louder, and unapologetically proclaim their next steps. Sometimes, like Anne back in the introduction, they don't even know what's happening. They just see ten times more money coming in and overlook the fact that they're now telling people no, asking important questions, and taking back control of their business—and, really, their life. They have found *their* confidence, and now it's time for you to find *yours*.

Now you never have to miss another family dinner, be late for the five o'clock soccer game, or decide between laundry or payroll. You can live life on your own terms because you have confidence in your ability to run your business. You no longer lose sleep over three providers quitting back-to-back because you have a way to treat that problem. You no longer consider sinking thousands into an ad campaign because you've had a similar diagnosis once before, and the treatment interventions worked beautifully. It's about more than just treating your business like a patient; it's about knowing *it's all going to be okay*.

At the end of a long, hard day, I just want you to remember one thing: Because of your background and training as a healthcare professional, you are perfectly suited to run this business. After all, it is like a patient, and you just have to treat it that way. When all else fails, go back to what you know. You know how to treat people. You know how to instill hope. You know how to give patients actionable steps in order for them to achieve wellness. You know how to structure a treatment plan and you know how to troubleshoot when things aren't going the way you had hoped.

You know how to do this. I want you to go out there and find your inner Lillie, using those cotton flour sacks to patch together the entrepreneurial confidence that is waiting for you to wear it proudly. That little house in Fonthill, Kentucky, no longer stands, but what it stood for does. Although we focused on **SALES**, **PROFIT**, and **ORDER** in this book, **IMPACT** and **LEGACY** have been here all along.

That little house, wedged behind the bigleaf magnolia, represents the legacy we all hope to leave behind. Not because of the lumber or because it had any monetary value, but because it was the foundation from which my family grew. Although I never got to see it, I can feel a connection to what it did. It raised my granny Lillie up strong; it provided the opportunity for that baby to be born in the back of the Ford, who then went on to become my mom. If it weren't for that house and those circumstances, I wouldn't be here telling you this story now. I wouldn't have the opportunity to impact your life through my experience, or leave the legacy I want to leave.

Like that magnolia, my roots are strong. I find strength in my family's history, their stories, and knowing what they had to overcome. It will take more than some business problems to bring me down, and the same goes for you. If they did it, then so can we. We tell our patients this all the time. We remind them of it at every session, and we plaster it on our walls as a reminder. We can do this. You can do this. Practice what you preach, dear reader, and you will be as strong as that magnolia and impactful as that little house; you will leave a legacy, like Granny Lillie did.

Acknowledgments

It's hard to write these acknowledgments without the cactus (me) getting a little emotional. I should start by saying thank you to my husband, Trevor, who is a lighthouse. Without him, nothing I do would be possible. He takes care of our children while I work, he runs the roads, and he puts up with my sassiness. Trevor, you were my support when I was *just* a therapist, you built me up as an entrepreneur, and now we start this new journey together as I officially call myself an author. You have been my rock, my cheerleader, and the one who makes me laugh at your inability to pronounce words correctly. Your encouragement is priceless, and if it weren't for you, I would never be in a position to help others because I would still need help myself. You brought me out of a darkness I didn't even know I was in. And I love you.

I want to follow that up with a big shout-out to my team at Mindsight Behavioral Group, who make everything I do bearable and, most of the time, fun. There's no way to name all of you, but every single one of you holds a special place in my heart. Shona, you're the most loyal therapist and friend anyone could ever have. Tonya, Hunter, and Tracy, I see you. I appreciate you, too.

I poke lots of fun at Jackie and her love for dashboards and donuts throughout this book, but Jackie, you're our needle in a haystack: rare, hard to find, but packing a hard punch. Literally. I have the bruises to prove it. You have been a game-changer for my company, and for that I will be eternally grateful. Badass Britany, you're not too shabby either. Your eagerness to learn and your determination to help others are contagious. You've been instrumental in my efforts to get Mindsight where it is today. Anita, you as well. You may just be the most loyal person I have ever met. I appreciate everything you have done for me.

Emily, I can't thank you enough for fixing my daily technology catastrophes and working with me to launch this book in a big way. You huff and puff sometimes, but you always keep me on track and manage all the techy stuff that is to blame for my gray hairs (while providing the Mary Kay to help keep them at bay).

I guess I should thank the pirate, the penny, and my dear granny Lillie for the compass. We all find ourselves up to our eyeballs in bullshit every now and then, so I'm not unique in that way, but knowing we're not alone makes it a little more bearable. If it wasn't for the pirate, I wouldn't have had the opportunity to humble myself so early on—enabling me to find *my entrepreneurial confidence* so I could tell every pirate that came after to kiss my ass. If it weren't for the pirate, I would have never been given that penny, which is still taped to my adding machine. It now represents the support I've been blessed with in my company, from employees whom I also call my friends.

I have to thank Mike Michalowicz and AJ Harper for their support. AJ, I consider you a rare second lucky penny. You came along when I least expected it, at a point where my dream of becoming an author was still just a dream. If you're reading this, I'm sure you'll say, "Kasey Compton, you didn't need luck, but I'll give it to you anyway."

My response: "AJ, I'll take anything I can get." I'm thirty-six years old right now, and you are the first person who ever told me, "You have God-given talent." I know you meant it when you said it, and I will not let you down.

Granny Lillie, I know you're watching. You deserve your own book, but that's for another day. You are a part of me now and will be for the rest of my life. Even after that, you'll be a part of my daughters because that's just how strong a woman you were. That's how strong I want to be. Just so you know, your internal compass didn't end with you. You left a legacy, sweet lady. You made an impact on my life and so many others. I don't think I ever told you that I loved you, but I did, and I still do.

As silly as it may sound, I feel compelled to thank the band NEEDTOBREATHE for sharing their talent and inspiring others like me with their art. NEEDTOBREATHE, I listened to your music as I wrote every single word in this book. I never feel more alive than when I breathe in the summer air, feel the heat beneath my feet, and blast your music in my ears. Your lyrics created the space I needed to think clearly, deeply, and with meaning to compose this manuscript. As I make my last editing pass, I can feel the mood of your music in my tone, and your rhythm in my prose.

Last but not least, I want to honor my roots, where I came from, Somerset, Kentucky. It's where I was born and the place I always come back to. Although Kentucky has my heart, it has to be said that South Carolina has stolen my soul. As I sit here in the exact spot on Fripp Island where I started this book, I write the last few words too. I look around at the palms and pines, taste the salt of the ocean, feel the heat of the sun, and crave more of the inspiration you always seem to give me.

Here we are, down to the last few words of *Fix This Next for Healthcare Providers,* and it's kind of sad—like the feeling I get every time I cross the drawbridge to leave the island and head back to Kentucky. But just as I remind myself every time that "This place isn't going anywhere," I also remind myself that while this was my first book, it will not be my last.

Hey, Michalowicz, it's about that time. We started this book with a toast, so it would only be right to end with one too. Excuse me for a moment while I crack open a bottle, pour a glass of Pappy Van Winkle 23 Year—neat—and celebrate all of us entrepreneurs and our accomplishments. Until next time, y'all. Cheers!

ABOUT THE AUTHOR

Kasey Compton is a spirited entrepreneur who has embraced all the road-blocks that come with being a business owner and loves using her experiences to help others. Kasey designed her mental health practice, Mindsight Behavioral Group, to be highly recognizable, community-focused, *and*

profitable. Recently featured in Mike Michalowicz's *You've Got This* magazine, Mindsight Behavioral Group went from zero to three million dollars in less than three years and continues to grow today, with a plan to dominate the world!

Kasey's ability to combine analytical and creative skills has proven successful in her consulting firm, where she helps people navigate their entrepreneurial journey. Her specialties include cutting through the clutter to pinpoint the right problem, increasing efficiency, and tapping into a person's highest potential. Kasey designed her company to provide the map that guides business owners through the entrepreneurial process. Always comfortable charting her own course, Kasey has a gift for envisioning possibilities that allows her to generate a wealth of new ideas when others find themselves stuck. People often ask her, "How on earth did you come up with that?"

Kasey welcomes opportunities that allow her to reach others and broaden her impact, such as presenting onstage, speaking from behind the mic as a podcast guest, and sharing stories through her business books. She is passionate about connecting and engaging with others, as she feels her purpose in life is to help business owners find their entrepreneurial confidence. (Here's the secret: *it was there all along!*) Kasey believes that in business, as in any journey, the destination is important, but what you find along the way is what matters most.

Find her online:
Facebook: @hikaseycompton
Instagram: @hikaseycompton
Twitter: @KaseyCompton

WWW.KASEYCOMPTON.COM

CPSIA information can be obtained
at www.ICGtesting.com
Printed in the USA
LVHW090759110721
692392LV00004B/344

9 781736 211908